Prospects for Tomc

Tomorrow's Biodiversity

Tomorrow's Biodiversity

Vandana Shiva

Thames & Hudson

Any copy of this book issued by the publisher as a paperback is sold subject to the condition that it shall not by way of trade or otherwise be lent, resold, hired out or otherwise circulated without the publisher's prior consent in any form of binding or cover other than that in which it is published and without a similar condition including these words being imposed on a subsequent purchaser.

First published in the United Kingdom in 2000 by Thames & Hudson Ltd, 181A High Holborn, London WC1V 7QX

© 2000 Vandana Shiva

All Rights Reserved. No part of this publication may be reproduced or transmitted in any form or by any means, electronic or mechanical, including photocopy, recording or any other information storage and retrieval system, without prior permission in writing from the publisher.

British Library Cataloguing-in-Publication Data
A catalogue record for this book is available from the British Library

ISBN 0-500-28239-0

Printed and bound in Slovenia by Mladinska Knjiga

CONTENTS

PREFACE

I was trained as a physicist and had imagined my life would be passed in the company of elementary particles. Instead, I have spent the last twenty-five years with forest species and crop varieties and with the farmers who have conserved the amazing diversity of plants and animals. In the past two decades I have been trying to understand why so many of our fellow creatures are being pushed to extinction, why more and more people are permanently hungry in spite of technologies that are supposed to increase food production, why farmers are being dispossessed and pushed into debt by economic models that are supposed to improve their incomes and create prosperity.

Philosophically my training as a quantum physicist has been helpful in trying to address some of these complex issues. While the classical physics of Descartes and Newton presented the world as atomized, isolated, immutable entities, quantum theory reframed the world as constantly changing and inseparable systems in dynamic interaction, with indeterminate potentials rather than with unchanging properties with fixed outcomes.

It is these qualities of inseparability and indeterminacy that guide my approach to natural systems and the human impact on the environment. I have looked at biodiversity in the inter-relationship between species, and between genetic structures and their context.

Through the lens of biodiversity, the world looks different and demands a change in the dominant concepts of technology and trade. Such a shift is necessary for sustainability. I would, in fact, say that biodiversity is the indicator of sustainability – the more we can conserve it, the more sustainable our actions are – the more we destroy it, the more non-sustainably we are living.

What is the future of biodiversity? Uncertainty is another legacy of quantum theory. The future of biodiversity is as uncertain as the future of the human species and the future of society. There are many initiatives and processes underway for the conservation of biodiversity, from local actions to global treaties (such as the Convention on Biological Diversity signed at Rio at the Earth Summit in 1992). On the other hand, the destruction of biodiversity is simultaneously expanding and accelerating. The worldwide spread of industrial agriculture through the forces of globalization, including the trade liberalization rules of the World Trade Organization are leading to a rapid erosion of diversity.

In 1992, the conservation of biodiversity was the dominant trend. By 1995, with the elevation of the trade rules of WTO above environmental treaties and national laws, the destruction of diversity had started to appear inevitable. In 1999, that inevitability was challenged with the protests at Seattle. Alternatives became possible to imagine globally, not just locally – alternatives that paid attention to the needs of people and our non-human kin, and were not pre-occupied with trade and profits.

But there is no certainty about which trend will shape our future and the future of biodiversity. Will greed win or will compassion survive? Only the future can tell.

WHAT IS BIODIVERSITY AND WHY IS IT IMPORTANT?

Biodiversity means the diversity of life – the rich diversity of life forms on our beautiful planet. Biodiversity is the very fabric of life – it provides the conditions for life's emergence and maintenance, and the many different ways in which that life is expressed. Biological diversity and cultural diversity are intimately related and interdependent. Biodiversity is in fact the embodiment of centuries of cultural evolution, because humans have co-evolved with other species in the diverse ecosystems of the world. Biodiversity in its turn has shaped the world's diverse cultures. The erosion of biodiversity and the erosion of cultural diversity are related. Both have been threatened by the globalization of an industrial culture based on reductionist knowledge, mechanistic technologies and the commodification of resources.

Throughout the twentieth century it was considered that substitutes could be found for resources supplied by biodiversity: renewable sources of energy – wood and animal energy – could be replaced by fossil fuel; manure for growing food could be replaced by the products of fertilizer factories; and medicines could be made from synthetic molecules. But fossil fuels have given us climate change; agrichemicals have threatened species, undermined soil fertility and human health; and synthetic drugs have had fatal side-effects.

People everywhere are looking for alternatives that will conserve our fellow beings and produce sustainable solutions for human health and nutrition. Biodiversity and cultural diversity hold the key to these sustainable alternatives. Around the world organic agriculture is again in favour and on the increase, and alternative medicine, inspired by Chinese, Indian and other indigenous knowledge systems is gaining popularity even in the West.

However, while the movement for the rejuvenation of bio-cultural diversity is growing, new threats are emerging. Economic globalization is rapidly expanding biological and social monocultures, pushing out the diversity that remains. New technologies, such as genetic engineering, are creating new risks of biopollution while increasing chemical pollution.

The destruction of biodiversity translates into the destruction of the diversity of the livelihoods of the large majority of Third World people who make their living as farmers, fishermen, craftspeople and healers. The diversity of life forms is also fast becoming the 'green oil' or raw material for the next industrial revolution based on the emerging biotechnologies. Industry is reorganizing itself as the 'life sciences' industry, changing property laws, environmental laws and trade policies to create markets for genetically engineered products and to establish monopolies in the vital sectors of food and medicine.

Different approaches to scientific knowledge raise fundamentally different problems and give fundamentally different answers to basic questions about the nature of biological organisms, their functions and values, their economic utility, and the impact of genetically engineered organisms on people's health and the environment. Reductionist biology is in conflict with relational biology. The reductionist approach is characterized by the assumption that organisms are mechanical constructs made of genes, their functions are determined by genes and life forms are 'gene machines' that can be redesigned to perform new functions. It provides the basis of genetic engineering and the patenting of life. If organisms are merely bundles of DNA, shuffling DNA around is like moving bricks around in house construction, or moving machine parts in automobiles.

The Erosion of Biodiversity

At the Earth Summit at Rio de Janeiro in 1992, the Convention on Biological Diversity was drawn up. It provides a comprehensive definition of the term biological diversity, which it defines under Article 2 as: 'The variability among living organisms from all sources including *inter alia*, terrestrial, marine and other aquatic ecosystems and the ecological complexes of which they are a part; this includes diversity within species, between species and ecosystems.' Estimates of the number of species in existence vary from 3.6 million to 100 million, of which, to date, scientists have described an estimated 1.7 million. According to present counts, bacteria have 3,058 recognized species; vascular plants have 260,000; fungi have 70,000; viruses have 500,000; vertebrates have 45,000; and insects have 950,000.

All life forms have an intrinsic worth and a right to evolve freely on their own terms. Humankind is one among millions of other species. It does not have a right to push other species to extinction, or to manipulate them for greed, profit and power without concern for their wellbeing. Compassion for all living things has been the basis of most ancient faiths in the world, and is the basis of contemporary movements for animal welfare, for wilderness protection and for the conservation of biodiversity. Native Americans refer to other species as brothers and sisters. In India we think in terms of the Earth Family.

For agribusiness, the biotechnology industry and the technicians who serve them, however, other species have value only as sources of raw material and profit, and can be manipulated and engineered regardless of their welfare. For instance, cows are just udders for the maximization of milk production using recombinant bovine growth hormones (rbgh). Sheep are 'mammalian bioreactors' for the production of pharmaceuticals in their mammary glands. Microbes and plants are sources of genes and provide substances which can be extracted, recombined with other organisms, patented, and bought and sold in global markets.

The ethical conflict between the intrinsic worth and the commercial value of all life forms has become a major issue in negotiations at the World Trade Organization (WTO), in the commercialization of genetic engineering of plants and animals, and in the patents taken out around the world on plants, animals and microorganisms. In Seattle where the WTO met for trade talks in 1999, in Washington at the World Bank meeting in April 2000, in Davos at the World Economic Forum, and in Millau at José Bové's trial for attacking McDonald's in

July 2000, thousands of people took part in protests to call attention to the rights and the inherent value of other species.

Seeing other life forms as biological and genetic raw material is fraught with ecological risks. The smallest microbe plays a critical role in maintaining the ecological processes that create the conditions of life for all species, including, of course, our own. Our ignorance of the ecological functions of diverse forms of life is no excuse for us to push species to extinction, or to manipulate them without concern for the ecological impact. Species now become extinct at the rate of 27,000 per year – 1,000 times the natural rate – and human greed and desire for profit are the primary cause of most of these extinctions.

Biodiversity, from genes to species to ecosystems, works in harmony and in concert to create and maintain life. This is at the heart both of ancient wisdom and of new holistic theories, such as James Lovelock's 'Gaia' theory, which is, in summary, that the earth is a living system, self-regulating and self-organizing. Just as our bodies maintain their temperature, the earth's equilibrium is maintained through ecological processes in which biodiversity plays a central role.

Biodiversity is assessed at three fundamental levels of biological organization: genetic, species and ecosystem diversity.

Genetic diversity is the variation at the genetic level, i.e. in the components of nucleic acids which constitute the genetic code. Genes are considered the blueprints of life. While gene theory is elegant for understanding replication and inheritance, it is totally inadequate when extended to a theory of life. Only one per cent of all the genetic material of higher organisms is known to relate to the form and function of the organism. We are still ignorant about the role of the remaining 99 per cent, but, in our usual human arrogance, instead of referring to our 99 per cent ignorance, we refer to the 99 per cent 'junk' DNA. In any case, the complex functions and traits of biological systems cannot be reduced to the genetic level. As the eminent molecular biologist, Professor Richard Strohman of Berkeley, has stated:

Neither genes nor environments 'cause' complex traits. If a word is needed there, then 'cell' will name the cause. It is the cell, and the body of cells as a whole, that selects from the dynamical interactions inherent in its physical and chemical pathways, and responds formatively and adaptively to the external environment. We have mistakenly replaced the concept and reality of the cell as a dynamical center of integrative activity with the concept of gene causality.

(Interview in *Wild Duck Review*, Summer 1999)

Reducing biodiversity to the genetic level is therefore ecologically and scientifically misguided. The value and functions of living organisms are important at higher levels of organization.

Species diversity is the species richness of an ecosystem – the word species literally means outward or visible form. All cultures have ways of organizing life forms along lines of difference. The ecological significance of species can vary tremendously. A tree of the tropical rainforest can support more than a hundred species of insects, whereas a European alpine plant may have no other species wholly dependent on it.

Ecosystems are ecologically and biologically organized systems consisting of diverse flora and fauna. Since an ecosystem is an ecological unit by definition, a simple arithmetical count of variation is not enough to assess biodiversity. Ecological interactions between diverse species become the key measure for ecosystem diversity. Tropical rainforests are the richest terrestrial ecosystems. They cover 7 per cent of the world's surface area, and may well contain 70 per cent of all species (Groombridge, ed., *Global Biodiversity*, 1992). Oceans occupy two-thirds of the Earth's surface, and, although they are as rich as forest ecosystems, they have been viewed as 'a vast desert, desperately short of nutrients and with living things spread most thinly through them' (Colinvaux, *Why Big Fierce Animals are Rare*, 1980).

For the first 2 billion years of the 3.5 billion years or more that life has existed, bacteria and other microorganisms were the only living things on earth. As the famous geneticist David Suzuki says in *From Naked Ape to Super Species* (1999), 'We owe practically all life to bacteria.' Microorganisms create the planet's living environment which supports life. According to James Lovelock, photosynthetic cyanobacteria were instrumental in producing oxygen, without which human life would not be possible. Microorganisms continue to play a critical role in maintaining biogeochemical cycles. The recycling of water, oxygen, methane, carbon dioxide, nitrogen, sulphur and carbon is made possible by diverse species working incessantly to maintain the ecological processes that support life. Forty per cent of the carbon fixed by photosynthesis is carried out by algae and cyanobacteria in the seas and oceans. Fungi that decay wood release about 85 billion tonnes of carbon as CO_2 into the atmosphere each year. Each year, bacteria fix 240 million tonnes of nitrogen, release 210 million tonnes of nitrogen by denutrification and release 75 million tonnes of ammonia (Groombridge (ed.), *Global Biodiversity*, 1992). The work of micro-organisms reduces industrial activity to insignificance.

The greatest biomass in soil, on the basis of current evidence, is that of the microorganisms, above all the fungi. Soil microorganisms maintain soil structure, contribute to the biodegradation of dead plants and animals, and fix nitrogen, and so are the key to soil fertility. Their destruction by chemicals threatens our survival and our food security. When scientists in Denmark scooped up a cubic metre (35 cubic feet) of earth from a beech forest and took it into their laboratory, they found 50,000 small earthworms, 50,000 insects and mites, and 12 million roundworms. A gram of the same soil revealed 30,000 protozoa, 50,000 algae, 400,000 fungi and billions of individual bacteria of 4,000 unknown species.

Bacteria, fungi and protozoa in the guts of animals perform crucial functions in digestion, without which the so-called higher animals could not exist. Microorganisms are also powerful factors in disease and death.

In the oceans, which are so central to the maintenance of Gaia's life, up to 80 per cent of the biomass and productivity in open waters is contributed by ultra planktonic algae (Anderson, 'The Diversity of Eukaryotic Algae', in *Global Biodiversity*, 1992).

Human beings are clearly highly ignorant of other members of the Earth Family and, at least in the Western worldview, have thought of themselves as sitting on top of a biodiversity pyramid or tree rather than forming a part of a complex web of life. Even the most popular conservation programmes have focused on the species closest to human beings, the large mammals: 'Project Tiger' and 'Project Elephant' have been the dominant models for biodiversity conservation. Microbes have had no conservation movements or campaigns for 'microbe rights' for their protection. Nor has it been recognized that in the final analysis microbes are more powerful than 'Man'.

The lesson from biodiversity is co-operation, not competition. It is that the big depends on the small, and cannot survive by exterminating the small.

Since ecological stability or instability is linked to species interactions, it is the relational approach to biodiversity that is important, not the arithmetical approach. For the same reason, conserving biodiversity cannot be achieved by putting it in a museum or a zoo. Biodiversity in balance creates the conditions of life, and species in conflict and out of balance become life-threatening.

I therefore follow the approach to biodiversity which is based not on the number of species or their variation, but takes account of the ecological web of life that species create in interaction. I differentiate between the arithmetical approach and the ecological approach. The arithmetical approach is currently the dominant one. It relates to 'variation or differences among some set of entities' – and 'number, variety and variability used to describe the number, variety and variability of living organisms' (Groombridge, ed., *Global Biodiversity*, 1992). The extinction of a species means not just the loss of that particular species, but also a threat to the other species that are supported by it through ecological processes. When one plant becomes extinct, with it disappear the twenty to forty animal and insect species that rely on it. Salmon, which spend their adult lives at sea, return to their natal streams to spawn. Bears, eagles and wolves catch the salmon and transfer the nutrients to the land. Marine carbon and nitrogen isotopes in salmon have been tracked by scientists, and 25–40 per cent of the carbon and nitrogen in juvenile salmon was found to come from their parents. Ninety per cent of the nitrogen and carbon in the bodies of grizzly bear was of marine origin. A single bear will catch 750 salmon, of which the partially consumed carcasses become nutrients for trees. Salmon are the biggest source of nitrogen fertilizer for the forest thousands of miles from the ocean. The growth of trees is correlated to the marine carbon and nitrogen the salmon bring to the forest. As David Suzuki says in giving this beautiful example of the web of life, 'The fish need the forest, the forest needs the fish' (*From Naked Ape to Super Species*). This interrelationship and mutual dependence is the reason why biodiversity cannot be looked at in a fragmented, atomized context.

Mass extinctions have taken place during geological time, but the erosion of biodiversity has become a systemic product of industrialization. For animals, habitat loss, caused by large dams, industrial plantations, highways and the expansion of human settlements, is the major threat to species survival. Species of birds and fish have also been pushed to extinction by the use of pesticides; this was the story of Rachel Carson's *Silent Spring* (1965). In 1998, the British Trust for Ornithology (BTO) published a major review of the conservation status of breeding birds since 1992. Twenty species were placed on the BTO's 'high alert' list owing to severe population declines of over 50 per cent in the last twenty-five years (Crick, et al., *Breeding Birds in the Wider Countryside*). A press release of 21 March 1999 by the Royal Society for the Protection of Birds (RSPB) stated that three-quarters of the UK's skylarks – that is 4.6 million – have vanished as a consequence of pesticide use.

According to the International Union for the Conservation of Nature (IUCN), 1,029 birds, 1,083 insects, 507 mammals, 169 reptiles, 57 amphibians, 713 fish, 409 molluscs, 154 corals and sponges, 139 annelid worms and 126 crustaceans are threatened. In terms of percentages, 11.7 per cent of the mammal species, 10 per cent of the birds, 3.67 per cent of the fish and 3.5 per cent of the reptiles are threatened.

Globalization has accelerated the destruction of biodiversity to such a pace and on such a scale that plants and animals that were common a few years ago have disappeared. Global market integration converts millions of acres of forests and farms into industrial monocultures, displacing and destroying both biodiversity and the cultural diversity of local communities.

According to the dominant paradigm of production, diversity goes against productivity, which creates an imperative for uniformity and monocultures. The irony of modern plant- and animal-breeding is that it destroys the very building blocks on which the technology depends. Forestry development schemes introduce monocultures of industrial species, such as eucalyptus, and push into extinction the diversity of local species that fulfils local needs. The Leipzig Global Plan of Action on Plant Genetic Resources for Food and Agriculture, 1995, based on 158 country reports and 12 regional and sub-regional papers, stated that 'the chief contemporary cause of the loss of genetic diversity has been the spread of modern, commercial agriculture'. Agricultural modernization schemes introduce new and uniform crops into farmers' fields and destroy the diversity of local varieties. In the words of Professor Garrison Wilkes of the University of Massachussetts, this is analogous to taking stones from the foundation of a building in order to repair the roof. Monocultures are ecologically unstable – this alone should be enough to prevent them being viewed as essential to production. The narrowing of the genetic base of agriculture leads to increased vulnerability of production and a threat to food security. Growing uniformity is increasing the risk of crop failure. The imperative to destroy diversity in order to increase productivity comes from a one-dimensional monoculture paradigm which fails to take the diverse functions of diverse species into account. Some of these functions include ecosystem maintenance. Destruction of diversity encourages pests and diseases. More than 70,000 pest species destroy 40 per cent of the world's harvest. During the past forty years, crop loss to insects alone has nearly doubled, despite a tenfold increase in the amount of pesticides applied (Pimental, et al., in *Bio-Science*, December 1997).

Biodiversity has rescued our food security from the risks of genetic uniformity. Wheat breeders used *T. monococcum*, macaroni wheat, for its resistance to rust, caused by *Puccima* fungi. Rust epidemics can destroy 75 per cent of the crop, and even in normal years it causes losses of 4 per cent or 2.3 million tonnes (Prescott-Allen, *Genes from the Wild*, 1983). During the 1970s, grassy stunt virus destroyed more than 116,000 hectares (290 acres) of rice in Indonesia, India, Sri Lanka, Vietnam and the Philippines. It is controlled by introducing resistance from the wild rice species *Oryza nivara*. If this wild rice had not been collected and saved in India, the food security of millions would have been threatened. Of the 6,000 varieties screened, only the wild rice from India had resistance to the disease. Similarly, wild maize varieties have the potential of saving $50–250 million dollars' worth of the maize crop in the USA from disease.

The potato famine in Ireland in 1845–46 was caused by genetic uniformity which led to an epidemic of potato blight, caused by the fungus *Phyto plithora infestans*. The famine reduced Ireland's population from 8.2 million in 1841 to 6.2 million in 1851. Future potato famines were prevented by wild potato varieties from the Andes. Traditional cultures have conserved biodiversity, and this is why it is still available for the rescue of industrial monocultures each time they became vulnerable to disease and pests.

A 1972 National Academy of Sciences study, 'The Genetic Vulnerability of Major Crops', stated: 'The corn crop fell victim to the epidemic because of a quirk in the technology that had designed the corn plants of America, until, in one sense, they had become as alike as identical twins. Whatever made one plant susceptible made them all susceptible.' (Doyle, *Altered Harvest*, 1985.)

As the food industry becomes more concentrated and integrated, uniformity is the result, and the globalization of consumption patterns, by creating monocultures and destroying diversity, has a devastating effect on the poorest on the planet. First, they are pushed into deeper poverty by being forced to 'compete' with globally powerful forces to gain access to the local biological resources. Secondly, their economic alternatives outside the global market are destroyed.

A US Department of Agriculture list of recommended fruits published in 1897 included more than 275 different varieties of apples. Today the apple varieties sold are less than a dozen. Supermarkets around the world essentially offer three types of apples: a red one, the

Starking, from the USA; a yellow one, the so-called Golden Delicious, also from the USA; and a green one, the Granny Smith or pippin, from Australia (Vellvé, *Saving the Seed*, 1992). A survey in France showed that a few years ago, the diet was rich with 250 plant species including vegetables, fruits and condiments. Today, barely 60 are cultivated in that country, and of these only 30 make up the bulk of local consumption. Crop genetic resources are disappearing at the rate of 1–2 per cent per annum (UN Food and Agriculture Organization, FAO, Development Education Exchange Papers, September 1993). About 75 per cent of the diversity of agricultural crops is estimated to have been lost since the beginning of the century.

Globally, domestic livestock breeds are disappearing at an annual rate of 5 per cent or 6 breeds per month (FAO, World Watch List for Domestic Animal Diversity, 5 December 1995). Of 4,000–5,000 breeds, 1,500 are threatened with extinction.

There is considerable evidence globally that the trend is towards monoculture and uniformity and away from diversity:

- In the European Union:
  75 per cent of the milk is produced by a quarter of the dairy farms;
  80 per cent of the pork comes from 10 per cent of the pig farms;
  90 per cent of the poultry comes from 10 per cent of the poultry farms;
  60 per cent of the cereals come from 6 per cent of the arable farms.
- In Europe 80 per cent of all farmland is sown to just four crops.
- In the Netherlands:
  a single potato variety covers 80 per cent of potato-growing land;
  three wheat varieties cover 90 per cent of wheat-growing land.
- In the UK:
  three varieties of potatoes make up 68 per cent of the crop;
  one variety makes up the remaining 32 per cent.
- In Greece, wheat diversity has declined by 95 per cent.
- In India, under the impact of the Green Revolution, rice varieties cultivated decreased from more than 100,000 to 10.
- In Sri Lanka, 2,000 varieties of rice were cultivated in 1959, but only 5 major varieties today.

- In India, 50 per cent of the goat breeds, 20 per cent of the cattle breeds and 30 per cent of the sheep breeds are in a danger of disappearing.
- The entire pork economy of the world is based on 4 breeds.
  In China 40 to 50 breeds were once farmed, and are now being replaced by hybrid pigs bred from the 4 'global' breeds.
- The world's main fishing grounds are being fished beyond their limits. About 70 per cent of the world's conventional marine species are threatened.
- One-fifth of all freshwater fish species known in the 1970s are already extinct or endangered.

The Wealth of the Poor

Biodiversity is not just a conservation issue, it is an issue affecting economic survival. Biodiversity is the means of livelihood and the 'means of production' of the poor who have no access to other assets or means of production. For food and medicine, for energy and fibre, for ceremony and crafts the poor depend on the wealth of biological resources and on their knowledge and skills related to biodiversity. As biodiversity disappears, the poor are further impoverished and deprived of the healthcare and nutrition that biodiversity provides. The consumption patterns of the rich and the production patterns of the powerful can undermine the consumption patterns of the poor by contributing to the erosion of biodiversity.

Agricultural biodiversity is the basis of economic life for two-thirds of the world's population – those people who live in rural economies in the Third World. The diversity of crop varieties and animal breeds have been developed as a response to the diversity of different ecosystems. Rice varieties have been developed to grow in flooded regions and in rainfed mountain slopes. Cattle breeds have been developed to match the climate in deserts and in wet rainforest regions.

There exists a very intricate relationship between local communities and biological diversity. Hunting-and-gathering communities use thousands of plants and animals for food, medicine and shelter. Pastoral, peasant and fishing communities have also developed the knowledge and skills to obtain a sustainable livelihood from living diversity, in both wild and domesticated forms, on the land, in the rivers, lakes and seas. The life of communities has been enhanced spiritually, culturally and economically as the communities in turn have enriched Earth's biodiversity.

All our food comes from wild species that have been domesticated and which need to return to their wild relatives to build genetic resistance to disease and pests. Approximately 80,000 edible plants have been used at one time or another since the beginning of agriculture, of which at least 3,000 have been used consistently. However, only about 150 have been cultivated. Globally we now rely on just eight crops to provide 75 per cent of the world's food.

India is rich in livestock. Breeds adapted to their specific local environmental and climatic conditions are indispensable to the rural economies of their regions. The animals provide draught power and transportation, dung as fertilizer and as cooking fuel, dairy products, wool, meat and leather. There are 26 breeds of cattle in India. The Ongole breed from Andhra Pradesh, excellent milkers, are also very strong, appropriate for heavy ploughing. The Desi from the same region, are hardy and disease-resistant, like the famous Vechur breed of Kerala, now on the brink of extinction. The Nagauri of the north are one of the most useful draught breeds in India, and the Red Sindhi cattle of Rajasthan are both good draught animals and sound milk producers. Rajasthan also possesses several breeds of camel, and of its eight breeds of sheep – six from the desert areas – the Nagra is the best wool producer. Sheep play a vital role in the rural economy providing wool, milk and meat. Tragically, many breeds are faced with extinction following a dramatic decline in their numbers over the last decades.

Over centuries, a delicate equilibrium has evolved between the indigenous animals and the flora of each region. The communities and their livestock are dependent on the wide range of fodder, and each species consumes different plants and trees so that a balance is sustained. A comprehensive medicinal knowledge of local plants has also developed to cure diseases in animals.

It has been estimated that three billion people – 60 per cent of the world's population – depend on traditional medicines as a principle source of cures for disease. In India and China, 80–90 per cent of traditional medicines are plant-based, and Chinese herbal treatments alone use 5,000 species. In Kenya, 40 per cent of herbal medicines come from the native forest trees. In Amazonia, an ethnobotanical team has catalogued more than 1,000 plants used by the Indian tribes, many of them as medicine. In South Africa, there are approximately 200,000 traditional healers. In total, about 3,000 species of higher plants are used for traditional medicines and of these about 300 are the most commonly used.

India has a rich and ancient heritage of medical knowledge based on its vast resources of medicinal plant biodiversity. India's medical system is called Ayurveda. Its earliest documentation is found in Aatharvaveda, one of the foremost ancient books of Indian knowledge, wisdom and culture, supposed to date from around 1500 BCE. These systems of knowledge and the sources from which they have evolved have survived millennia because they are built on sustainability. Even today, over 70 per cent of the health needs of India are met by these systems. According to an ethnobotanical survey, there are 7,500 species of plants used for medicinal purposes by local Indian communities.

India has something like 1,400 plants documented in various Ayurvedic texts, approximately 342 in Unani, and close to 328 in the Siddha system. This biodiversity-based traditional medicinal system is still being kept alive by 360,740 Ayurveda practitioners, 29,701 Unani experts and 11,644 specialists of Siddha, not to mention millions of housewives and elders who prepare homemade remedies for common ailments.

Everywhere local people have made independent appraisals of their local resources. The plant *Ephedra vulgaris,* which is found in trans-Himalaya, possesses broncho-dilation properties and is only found in that ecosystem. It is commonly used by the local people as a herbal tea, and taken several times a day. In Ayurveda (unlike most folk traditions, it is not oral but written down) there is a body of knowledge called *dhravya guna shastra,* which is the indigenous knowledge of pharmacology. Since the Vedic period a plant named tulsi (*Ocimum sanctum L.*) has had a very sacred place in Indian healing. In both Ayurveda and Siddha the tulsi leaves and the juices from its leaves, roots and seeds are used to cure various ailments, such as intestinal gas, coughs, worms, skin diseases and kidney disorders. It also regulates the flow of urine, subdues inflammation and restores the body by cleansing the system of toxins, while strengthening and toning every organ.

The Kani tribe of the Agastyar hills in Southern Kerala have a habit of eating the raw leaves of a plant known as arogya pacha (*Trichopus zeylnicus*), which they call 'health drug'. In the Central Himalayas, millet grain cooked in water is mixed with buttermilk and used in the treatment of chickenpox.

Quinine, digitalis and morphine are derived from plants, and even in the USA 40 per cent of all prescriptions still depend on natural sources. The first birth-control pills were made from a plant called *Diascorea*. Digitalis, the most popular medicine for heart problems, is made from *Digitalis* (foxglove) which contains glycosides, which regulate heart beats, in its leaves. Hypertension is treated by reserpine, derived from *Rauwolfia serpentia* which has been used in India for centuries. Quinine, for malaria, is basically an indigenous medicine from Peru. The tree was called quinaol quina-quina by the native Indians. From the rosy periwinkle, *Vinca rosea*, are extracted the cancer cures Vinblastine and Vincristine, and alkaloids derived from *Vinca rosea* are used for Hodgkin's disease and childhood leukemia (Koopowitz and Kaye, *Plant Extinction*, 1990).

It is estimated that 100 million of the world's poorest people depend on fishing for all or part of their livelihoods. According to an estimate by the FAO (UN Food and Agriculture Organization), there are a million large fishing boats and 2 million small boats. Most of the large fishing vessels are controlled by transnational corporations and use all the latest aids to fish-detection, catching and processing, allowing them to become more efficient hunting machines, and so leading to the problem of overfishing. As a special issue of the *Ecologist* reports, completely automatic trawlnets that detect the approach of a school of fish electronically, and automatically pay out or retrieve warp to place the net in the path of the shoal are now appearing on the market. The 'Gloria' super trawlnet, developed in Ireland, measures 110 by 170 metres (360 by 560 feet) at its mouth, large enough to swallow a dozen Boeing jumbo jets. The reduction of all value to commercial value results in the development of technologies which are ecologically crude. Large catches are made possible by the destruction of livelihoods and of diverse species. As a Malaysian community has said:

> The trawlers approved by the government 10 to 15 years ago are strongly opposed by the small inshore fishermen whose income is small and who use traditional nets. We should be concerned with the government's policy of too much dependence on modern science and technology...
> The root cause of the present scarcity of fish is trawler fishing. The trawler overturns the soil on the seabed and scoops up all the small fish and fry.

In India, ever since shrimp became an export commodity through export-oriented fisheries development, there is less to catch and less to eat. Until the end of the 1950s, the marine fish harvest increased at a rate of 5 per cent per annum. By the mid-'80s, after 'development', the rate of growth of the marine fish harvest had decreased. Fish consumption declined in India from 19 kg (42 lbs) per year *per capita* to 9 kg (20 lbs) per year.

From the early 1970s, landings of most of the major seabottom-dwelling fish began to decline sharply, largely because of excessive fishing (in the case of purseining) and destructive fishing (in the case of trawling which degraded the seabed). Catches of sardines and mackerel, once the mainstay of the fisheries, fell from 250,000 tonnes in 1968 to 87,000 tonnes in 1990. In this period in South America the consumption of fish went down by 7.9 per cent and in Africa by 2.9 per cent, while European fish consumption rose by 23 per cent.

This is the reason that small fishermen worldwide have organized as the World Forum of Fish Workers to protest for their right to fish. On 23 and 24 November 1994, a million fish workers from nine maritime states in India covering a coastline of over 7,500 kilometres (4,660 miles) went on strike. They were protesting against Indian government policies that gave international joint ventures free access to fish in the country's Exclusive Economic Zone (EEZ). During the week of the National Strike, one joint-venture vessel called at the port in Cochin, Kerala. Its hold contained 2,000 tonnes of perch and snapper, equivalent to the amount caught in one year by 1,000 hook-and-line fishermen in the region.

All the needs of two-thirds of the world's people are met by bio-diversity. If biodiversity is reduced, they are poorer. Even the privileged one-third of humanity living in the industrialized world depends on biodiversity. Oil and coal were made by creatures living millions of years ago. The cement that builds giant skyscrapers, bridges and parking lots comes from limestone, the remains of skeletons and shells, corals and other marine life.

While industrial civilization uses the gifts of biodiversity, it abuses the living richness of our world. The CO_2 pumped out by our energy and transportation systems is destabilizing climates, leading to an increase in forest fires, droughts, hurricanes, floods, and a rise in sea levels and sea temperature – all of which contribute to the loss of biodiversity. Industrial agriculture, forestry and fisheries convert rich, diverse ecosystems into biologically impoverished chemically inten-sive monocultures, writing a death sentence for millions of species while claiming higher 'growth'.

This is at the heart of the present conflicts over biodiversity. Systems that destroy biodiversity and those that conserve it both need it. In biodiversity-based economies it is the growth of biodiversity that is the measure of progress. In biodiversity-annihilating economies, it is the growth of money that is the measure of progress. We could, in fact, talk of systems that are life-centred and biodiversity-centred versus systems that are money- and capital-centred.

Rich and Poor in Biodiversity

When assessed in terms of biodiversity rather than financial capital, the South is rich and the North is poor. The wealth of Europe in the colonial era was, to a large extent, based on the transfer of biological resources from the colonies to the centres of imperial power, and the displacement of local biodiversity in the colonies by monocultures of raw material for European industry. The historian A. W. Crosby has called the biological transfer of wealth from the Americas to Europe the 'Columbian exchange', because with Columbus's arrival in America began the mass transfer of maize, potatoes, squash, tomatoes, peanuts, common beans, sunflowers and other crops across the Atlantic. Sugar, bananas, coffee, tea, rubber, indigo, cotton and other industrial crops were grown in new sites under the control of newly emerging colonial powers and their state-backed trading companies. The North accumulated wealth by gaining control over the biological resources of the South. Destroying the biodiversity that it could not use or control was the other less visible side of this process of colonization.

In spite of the immeasurable contribution that Third World biodiversity has made to the wealth of industrialized countries, corporations, governments and aid agencies of the North continue to create legal and political frameworks to make the Third World pay for what it originally gave. The emerging trends in global trade and technology work inherently against justice and ecological sustainability. They threaten to create a new era of bio-imperialism, built on the biological impoverishment of the Third World and the biosphere. Patents, industrialization of food and agriculture, globalization of trade through the rules of WTO are the new mechanisms by which the biological wealth of the South is being transferred to the North, leaving the Third World poorer both ecologically and economically.

The Empty Earth Syndrome

Third World countries located in the tropics have been endowed with great biological wealth and are the cradle of biodiversity. This wealth is being rapidly destroyed. In my view there are two root causes. The first arises from the 'empty-earth' paradigm of colonization, which assumes that ecosystems are empty if not taken over by Western industrial man or his clones. For five hundred years, colonization has been based on the idea of the 'emptiness' of the earth and of other cultures. The assumption of the empty land leads to the denial of prior inhabitants and their prior rights. The idea of emptiness also leads to the notion of limitlessness – that there are no limits set by nature or other cultures to be respected, no ecological or ethical limits, no limits to the level of greed or accumulation. The empty-earth hypothesis in addition creates a divided world – divisions which exist and deepen even in globalization, and were evident in the failed round of the WTO talks in Seattle. 'To us they cannot come, our land is full; to them we may go, their land is empty.' (Robert Cushman 1621, quoted in Kadir, *Columbus and the Ends of the Earth*, 1992.) Creating clones of Western forms of industrial production and excessive consumption is called 'development' but is actually 'maldevelopment'. (Shiva, *Staying Alive: Women, Ecology and Development*, 1998.) This view threatens other species and other cultures to extinction because it is blind to their existence, their rights and to the impact of the colonizing culture.

The second cause is what I have described as the monoculture of the mind: the idea that the world is or should be uniform and one-dimensional, that diversity is either disease or deficiency, and monocultures are necessary for the production of more food and economic benefits (Shiva, *Monocultures of the Mind*, 1993). It is the scientific and technological reflection of the empty-earth world-view. The shutting out of alternative ways of knowing and making leads to the assumption that the dominant knowledge and techniques are the only option. This monoculture of the mind destroys bio-diversity by blocking the perception of the multiple benefits and uses of biodiversity.

CHAPTER 1

THE EARTH FAMILY VS THE GENETIC MINE

There are two competing paradigms shaping the future of bio-diversity. The first is the ecological paradigm, which views humans as one among many species – as part of an Earth Family in which all members have an intrinsic value and are linked to each other in webs of reciprocal life support. It views all living organisms as complex, self-organized and constantly changing dynamic systems. Then there is the paradigm of the Genetic Mine. It views species, including human beings, merely as deposits of genes to be exploited by the new tools of genetic engineering. This paradigm is based on genetic reductionism, which reduces biology to genes and turns genes into commodities, ignoring the complexity of internal and external interactions that shape living systems. The hype for the 'genome map' is an example of the Genetic Mine idea – maps are made for prospecting for minerals, and the genome map is a guide to genetic mining. But, like maps of territory, genome maps do not tell the full story about life or biodiversity. To refer to the 'working draft' of 3.1 billion chemical letters of the human genome as the 'Book of Life', or to say with Bill Clinton 'Today we are learning the language in which God created life' is no longer science; it is a new mythology for reorganizing the biological world into raw material for the biotechnology industry. This reorganization also leads to the pirating of Third World resources and of indigenous knowledge, which are considered to acquire 'value' only when 'processed' into patentable commodities. It robs nature and cultures of their creativity. Diverse species and diverse cultures and knowledge systems are therefore destroyed, and they are pushed into extinction even as they are mined for the building of corporate empires.

The Earth Family paradigm is held by local communities, whose survival and sustenance are linked to the utilization and conservation of biodiversity. The Genetic Mine paradigm is held by commercial interests, whose profits are linked to the utilization of global biodiversity for large-scale, uniform, centralized and global production systems. For local indigenous communities, conserving biodiversity means conserving their rights to their resources and knowledge, and to their production systems based on biodiversity. For commercial interests, such as pharmaceutical and agricultural biotechnology companies, commercial production is based on the destruction of biodiversity.

As the tools of genetic engineering make it possible to move genes across species barriers, new property rights systems are emerging that allow biodiversity and its components to be 'owned' as 'intellectual property'. Since organisms with introduced genes have different ecological interactions within the organism and with the environment, genetic engineering also brings with it new ecological risks and new forms of pollution. These emergent trends are generating new conflicts about the ownership and use of biodiversity, about the new risks of biopiracy and biopollution.

Those who depend on biodiversity for survival know they must keep that diversity alive. Their economic values therefore merge with ecological values and the intrinsic value of each species. This is evident from the fact that in sustainable indigenous cultures, the species on whom humans depend most is a sacred species, held in reverence and conserved, even while being utilized for sustenance. In an industrial society there is no sacred and no intrinsic value of a species since this interferes with exploitation. Ecological values that generate the need for conservation and economic values that promote limitless exploitation are in conflict. Biodiversity is the centre of a clash of paradigms, worldviews and cultures. How these conflicts are resolved will determine the future of biodiversity and the future of humanity.

The Life Industry

Life, or biology, is capitalism's latest frontier. Corporations that made their profits selling chemicals are now reorganizing themselves. Global corporations are crossing the traditional boundaries of the pharmaceutical, biotechnology, agribusiness, food, chemicals, energy sectors and cosmetics to form the 'life sciences' industry. They are also merging with each other.

Monsanto, which used to be the fourth largest chemical company in the USA, has bought up seed and agricultural biotechnology companies across the world. It purchased Cargill's international seed operations in Central and Latin America, Europe, Asia and Africa. It took over Dekalb, the second largest corn company in the USA, and Holden, which controls 35 per cent of the corn seed market. Monsanto has bought up Agracetus and Calgene, which control broad patents on cotton, soya bean and mustard. It bought up Asgrow, a major soya company. It bought up leading seed companies in Brazil and India where it now has a major share in the hybrid seed market. As Robert Farley of Monsanto has said, 'What you're seeing is not just a consolidation of seed companies, it's really a consolidation of the entire food chain.' Monsanto has in its turn been bought up by Pharmacia.

Hoechst of Germany and Rhône Poulenc of France have merged to form Aventis, the largest Life Sciences Company, with combined sales of $20 billion per annum. Zeneca of the UK and Astra of Sweden have combined and have assets of $70 billion, higher than the Gross National Product of 93 of the world's developing countries. Dupont, the world's largest chemical company, has bought up Pioneer HiBreed, the world's largest seed company. According to Dupont's chairman, 'In the twentieth century, chemical companies made most of their products with non-living systems. In the next century, we will make many of them with living systems.'

Sandoz and Ciba Geigy merged to form Novartis. As Daniel Vasella, the CEO (Chief Executive Officer) of Novartis, has said, 'The common denominator of our business is biology. The research and technology is applied to discover, develop and sell products that have an effect on biological systems, be they human beings, plants or animals.' Plans have been made to merge the agribusiness units of Astra-Zeneca and Novartis to form Syngenta.

As erstwhile chemical companies combine to control the living resources of the planet, they also control the food and medicine sectors. Food and medicine are not just economic sectors – they are the very basis of the maintenance of human life. The poorer two-thirds of humanity provide for their own food and medicine through subsistence agriculture and indigenous medical systems. Without jobs, without bank accounts, without state welfare and unemployment insurance, they produce and reproduce life in partnership with biodiversity as nature's capital. The hijacking of the basis of life by the 'life industries' translates into a denial to the poor of their right to life. The creation of money as capital for corporations through control over biology is achieved by the destruction of nature as capital for the poor. Life as the process of biological survival is replaced by life as raw material and commodity, as 'Life Incorporated'.

There is, however, one problem with life from the point of view of capital. Life reproduces and multiplies freely. Living organisms self-organize and replicate. Life's renewability is a barrier to commodification. If life has to be commodified, its renewability must be interrupted and arrested. Converting biodiversity from a renewable resource, freely and perennially available to farmers and local communities, into a non-renewable commodity to be bought each year is achieved technologically through industrial breeding, and legally through patent and intellectual property rights.

Terminator Technology

To use Jack Kloppenburg's analogy of seed, it is both a 'means of production' as well as a 'product' (*First the Seed*, 1998). Whether indigenous peoples doing 'shifting cultivation' or peasants practising settled agriculture, in planting each year's crop the farmers also reproduce the necessary part of their means of production. The seed thus represents capital with a simple biological obstacle; given the appropriate conditions, it reproduces itself and multiplies, and is available free to the farmers each year.

Industrial breeding and genetic engineering are primarily tools for replacing the renewable abundance of life with scarce commodities, supplied at high cost by the seed corporations and the life-sciences industries. The cycle of regeneration is therefore replaced by a linear flow of free germplasm from farms and forests into corporate laboratories and research stations, and the flow of modified uniform products as priced commodities from corporations to farms and forests.

This change in the nature of biodiversity is exemplified in the case of seeds. New technologies treat self-regenerative seed as 'primitive' raw germplasm, and the seed that cannot reproduce and is inert without inputs (chemical fertilizers, pesticides, herbicides, fungicides, extra water) as a 'finished product'. The commodified seed is ecologically incomplete and ruptured at two levels:

1   It does not reproduce itself, while, by definition, seed is a regenerative resource. Through technological transformation, biodiversity is transformed from a renewable into a non-renewable resource.

2   It does not produce by itself. It needs the help of inputs to produce. As the seed and chemical companies merge, the dependence on inputs will increase, not decrease. Whether a chemical is added externally, as in the Green Revolution, or internally, as in the new biotechnologies, it remains an external input in the ecological cycle of the reproduction of seed.

On 3 March 1998 the US Department of Agriculture (USDA) and the Delta and Pine Land Company, the largest cotton seed company in the world, announced that they had jointly developed and received a patent on a new agricultural biotechnology. Benignly entitled, 'Control of Plant Gene Expression', the new patent will permit its owners and licensees to create sterile seed by cleverly and selectively programming a plant's DNA to kill its own embryos. The patent applies to plants and seeds of all species. The result? If saved at harvest for future crops, the seed produced by these plants will not grow. Pea pods, tomatoes, peppers and ears of wheat will essentially become seed morgues. Thus the system will force farmers to buy seed from seed companies each year. The system has been dubbed 'terminator technology' by groups such as the NGO, the Rural Advancement Foundation International (RAFI), which says that it threatens farmers' independence and the food security of over a billion poor farmers in Third World countries. While Monsanto announced that it would not use this technology, its attempts to buy Delta and Pine Land were unsuccessful, and the USDA and Delta and Pine Land continue to develop the technology to create sterile seeds.

Termination of germination is a means for capital accumulation and market expansion. However, abundance in nature and for farmers shrinks as markets grow for biotechnologists. When we sow seed, we say, 'May this seed be inexhaustible.' Biotechnologists, on the other hand, are in effect saying, 'Let this seed be terminated so that our monopoly is unchallenged and our profits are inexhaustible.'

Camila Montercinos, an agricultural scientist from Chile, has called terminator technology 'the neutron bomb of agriculture' and according to Geri Guidetti (RFSTE, *Monsanto*, 1998):

> Never before has man created such an insidiously dangerous, far-reaching and potentially 'perfect' plan to control the livelihoods, food supply and even survival of all humans on the planet. In one broad, brazen stroke of his hand, man will have irretrievably broken the plant-to-seed-to-plant-to-seed cycle, the cycle that supports most life on the planet. No seed, no food unless you buy more seed. The Terminator Technology is brilliant science and arguably 'good business', but it has crossed the line, the tenuous line between genius and insanity. It is a dangerous, bad idea that should be banned. Period....

As corporations merge, they use the tools of genetic engineering to alter the function and performance of plants and animals so that production is impossible without inputs that also have to be purchased from the corporations. For example, for herbicide-resistant crops both the seed and the herbicide have to be purchased from the same company, and the outputs are sold to the corporations for processing. The manipulation of output traits will allow the giant food-processing industry to control the food-production process totally, and make food merge with medicine through the engineering of 'nutriceuticals' – crops designed to produce medicine as well as nutrition.

This is of course not totally new. The Indian system of Ayurveda – the 'Science of Life' – views food as medicine. What is new about genetic engineering is that it *engineers* pharmaceutical traits into food, and hence does not use the natural healing properties of plants. Further, by engineering traits which can only be processed by large industry, it offers the possibility of total control over the production process. Farmers are reduced to 'hi-tech' slaves who have no creative or autonomous role in decisions about what is planted, how it is grown and where it is sold. According to a RAFI communiqué, 'they become renters of proprietary germplasm from the Gene Giants or their subsidiaries' (*Gene Giants*, March/April 1999).

Nature freely provides vitamin A in the biodiversity of plants. Nevertheless, funded by the Rockefeller Foundation, the Swiss government and the European Union, a Zurich research team has genetically engineered a new strain of rice by introducing three genes taken from a daffodil and a bacterium. This 'golden rice' therefore contains high levels of beta-carotene, which is converted into vitamin A within the body. According to the UN, more than two million children are at risk of going blind due to vitamin A deficiency. Golden rice has been proclaimed as a miracle cure for blindness, and a breakthrough in improving the health of billions of poor people, most of them in Asia.

More than $100 million have been spent over ten years to produce this transgenic rice. It will take millions more dollars and another ten years' development to produce varieties that can be grown in farmers' fields. But an easier, safer and less costly alternative to genetically engineered rice is to increase biodiversity in agriculture. The natural sources of vitamin A – liver, egg yolk, chicken, meat, milk, butter – might be out of the question for the poorest in Asia, but there are cheap sources of beta-carotene – carrots, dark-green leafy vegetables, pumpkin, mango, and so on. Women farmers in Bengal, for instance, grew over a hundred kinds of green leafy vegetable before the Green

Revolution's monocultures and herbicides destroyed much of the local plant biodiversity. These indigenous crops contribute to the whole web of local biodiversity, whereas the transgenic rice would push out not only traditional rice strains but also many other plant varieties. Local plants need less water (and less herbicides and pesticides) than the transgenic rice. Above all, since the vitamin A in golden rice is not naturally occurring and is genetically engineered, novel health risks posed by this form of the vitamin will need to be investigated before the rice is promoted by the International Rice Research Institute and aid agencies, or before it is commercialized.

Patents on Life

Living resources, the basis of life, constitute an ecological commons from which all species derive their life support. The living commons are now being enclosed. Plants, animals, microbes, cells, genes are being 'patented' and owned as 'intellectual property'. Patents are an exclusive right – or monopoly – given to an inventor to prevent others from making, exchanging, distributing, selling the patented product or products made through patented processes. Patents used to be restricted to industrial processes and did not cover biological processes and products.

The floodgates to patents on life were opened by genetic engineering. The first patent on life was given in 1980 to General Electric for a genetically modified bacterium. A patent is granted for an invention which is novel in a non-obvious manner. Anand Chakrabarty, the genetic-engineering scientist, admitted that he had created nothing new, he had merely shuffled genes around. The US Supreme Court interpretation was that genetically engineered organisms are a new 'manufacture' and a new 'composition of matter' and hence could be patented. An obsolete seventeenth-century metaphysics, the Cartesian mechanistic worldview, which treated the living processes of nature as dead and inert matter, was mobilized to create a new form of property – property in life – through claiming 'intellectual property rights' on microorganisms, plants, animals and even human cell lines. This has three serious implications.

Firstly, by claiming that moving genes from one organism to another amounts to 'making' and 'inventing' those organisms, a false claim to creation is being made. Living organisms make themselves. The introduction of a new gene does not amount to 'making' a new life form, or 'inventing' a new living organism. Movers of furniture cannot claim that they are builders of homes and their owners.

Secondly, patents create monopoly rights and increase the costs of food and medicine both by preventing Third World communities from producing their own seeds and medicine, and by raising the price, taking basic needs beyond people's access. The recent debate on AIDS therapies is related to patents. The Nobel Prize winning Médecins sans Frontières (MSF) has shown that a patented therapy costing $15,000 could be available for $200 without patents. Even if the pharmaceutical industry gives a 85 per cent concession, the therapy will cost $2,250.

Thirdly, a false claim to intellectual property rights is being made, appropriating the creativity of centuries of collective and cumulative innovation embodied in the biodiversity that humanity has used for food and medicine. Patents on life enable biopiracy.

IPRs (intellectual property rights) are supposed to be property rights to the products of the mind. If IPR regimes reflected the diversity of traditional knowledge that account for creativity and innovation in different societies, they would necessarily have to be plural, reflecting a triple plurality — of intellectual modes, of property systems, and of systems of combinations. But IPRs, as implemented nationally as a follow-up of the finalization of Uruguay Round of GATT (General Agreement on Tariffs and Trade) and the implementation of WTO rules, or as imposed unilaterally through Special Clause 301 of the US Trade Act, are a prescription for a monocultural knowledge. They are being used to universalize the US patent regime worldwide. This would inevitably lead to an intellectual and cultural impoverishment since it would displace other ways of knowing, other objectives for knowledge creation, and other modes of knowledge sharing.

The Trade Related Intellectual Property (TRIP) treaty of WTO is based on a highly restricted concept of innovation. By definition, it is weighted in favour of transnational corporations, and against citizens in general – Third World peasants and forest-dwellers in particular. People everywhere innovate and create. In fact, the poorest have to be the most innovative, since their daily survival depends on it. However, IPRs as construed in the trade treaty and as will be enforced by the WTO have been restricted and reduced at a number of levels.

Article 27.3 (b) of the TRIPs text refers to the patenting of life:

> Parties may exclude from patentability plants and animals other than microorganisms, and essentially biological processes for productions of plants or animals other than non-biological and microbiological processes. However, parties shall provide for the protection of plant varieties either by patents or by an effective *sui generis* system or by any combination thereof. This provision shall be reviewed four years after the entry into force of the Agreement.

On first reading, it appears that the article is about the exclusion of plants and animals from patentability. However, the words 'other than microorganisms' rules out the exclusion of microorganisms from patenting. Since microorganisms are living organisms, this is the beginning of a journey down the slippery slope that leads to the patenting of all life. Further, animals and plants are also patentable if microbiological and non-bioliogical techniques are used for their modification.

The issue of patent protection for modified life forms raises a number of unresolved political questions about ownership and control of genetic resources. The problem is that in manipulating life forms you do not start from nothing, but from other life-forms which belong to others – maybe through customary law.

Putting value on the gene through patents stands biology on its head. Complex organisms, which have evolved over millennia in nature, and through the contributions of Third World peasants, tribal peoples and healers, are reduced to their parts, and treated as mere inputs into genetic engineering. Patenting of genes thus leads to a devaluation of life forms by reducing them to their constituents and allowing them to be owned as private property. This reductionism and fragmentation might be convenient for commercial concerns but it violates the integrity of life as well as the common property rights of Third World peoples. On the basis of these false notions of genetic resources and their ownership through intellectual property rights, the rights of sovereign nations of the Third World are denied. The USA has accused Third World countries of engaging in 'unfair trading practice' if they fail to adopt US patent laws which allow monopoly rights in life forms. Yet it is the USA that has engaged in unfair practices in relation to the use of Third World genetic resources. It has freely taken the biological diversity of the Third World to spin millions of dollars of profits through patents, none of which have been shared with Third World countries. A wild tomato variety (*Lycopersicon chomrelewskii*) taken from Peru in 1962 has contributed $8 million a year to the American tomato-processing industry by increasing the content of soluble solids. Yet, none of these profits or benefits have been shared with Peru, the original source of the genetic material.

According to conservationists Robert and Christine Prescott-Allen, wild varieties contributed US$340 million per year between 1976 and 1980 to the US farm economy. The total contribution of wild germplasm to the American economy has been US$66 billion, which is more than the total international debt of Mexico and Philippines combined. This wild material is 'owned' by sovereign states and by local people (Wilson, ed., *Biodiversity*, 1986).

In the Genetic Mine paradigm, seeds that have been developed over millennia by nature and by farming communities are defined as 'raw material'. Farmers' seeds are rendered incomplete and valueless by the process that makes corporate seeds the basis of wealth creation. The indigenous varieties, evolved through both natural and human selection, and produced and used by Third World farmers worldwide, are called 'primitive cultivars'. Those varieties created by modern plant-breeders in international research centres or by transnational seed corporations are called 'advanced' or 'elite'. The tacit hierarchy in words like 'primitive' and 'elite' becomes explicit in the process of conflict. Thus, the North has always used Third World germplasm as a freely available resource and treated it as valueless. The advanced capitalist nations wish to retain free access to the developing world's storehouse of genetic diversity, while the South would like to have the proprietary varieties of the North's industry declared a similarly 'public' good. The North, however, resists this democracy based on the logic of the market. The Executive Secretary of IBPGR (International Bureau of Plant Genetic Resources) has argued that 'it is not the original material which yields cash returns'. A 1983 forum on Plant Breeding sponsored by Pioneer HiBreed stated that:

> Some insist that since germplasm is a resource belonging to the public, such improved varieties would be supplied to farmers in the source country at either zero or low cost. This overlooks the fact that 'raw' germplasm only becomes valuable after considerable investment of time and money, both in adapting exotic germplasm for use by applied plant breeders and in incorporating the germplasm into varieties useful to farmers.
>
> (Quoted by Jack Kloppenburg in *First the Seed*, 1988)

The corporate perspective sees as valuable only that which serves the market. However, all material processes also serve ecological needs and social needs, and these needs are undermined by the monopolizing tendency of corporations. Most Third World countries view genetic resources as common heritage. In most countries, animals and plants were excluded from the patent system until recently when the advent of biotechnologies changed concepts of ownership of life. The potential for gene manipulation reduces the organism to its genetic constituents. Centuries of innovation are totally devalued to give monopoly rights on life forms to those who manipulate genes with the new technologies, placing their contribution over and above the intellectual contribution of generations of Third World farmers for over ten thousand years in the areas of conservation, breeding, domestication and development of plant and animal genetic resources. As Pat Mooney has argued: 'The argument that intellectual property is only recognizable when performed in laboratories with white lab coats is fundamentally a racist view of scientific development.' ('From Cabbages to Kings', Proceedings of ICDA Conference on Patenting of Life Forms, Brussels, 1989.)

Two biases are inherent in this argument. One, that the labour of Third World farmers has no value, while the labour of Western scientists adds value. Secondly, that value is a measure only in the market. However, it is recognized that, the total genetic change achieved by farmers over the millennia was far greater than that achieved by the last hundred or two hundred years of more systematic science-based efforts.

The limits of the market system in assigning value can hardly be a reason for denying the high ecological and social value of farmers' and nature's seeds. It points more to the deficiency of the logic of the market than the status of the seed or the farmers' intellect. There is no justification for treating some germplasm as valueless and common heritage and another germplasm as a valuable commodity and private property.

The impact of patents on life and seed goes much further than rendering invisible the innovation of millions over millennia. They also convert a freely accessible common property of farmers and peasants into a commodity bought for every planting season. The creation of markets and corporate profits through patents and intellectual property is simultaneously the creation of poverty, debt and dependence for the poor. The injustice of this process is double since the biodiversity which is patented first came from Third World countries.

Patents and Biopiracy

Biodiversity and knowledge have been freely exchanged from community to community and from culture to culture. Free exchange has made everyone rich, intellectually and materially. However, the expansion of patents to cover life forms threatens to rob the poor of their wealth and of their primary capital for meeting health and nutrition needs.

Economic globalization has been accompanied by the growing phenomenon of 'biopiracy' – the patenting of indigenous knowledge and biodiversity. Patent and intellectual property rights systems are supposed to prevent piracy. In the area of biodiversity, they are in fact promoting biopiracy. Biopiracy takes place when knowledge from other cultures is taken freely, converted into patented 'intellectual property' with a right to deny people free access to that knowledge and to force them to pay royalties and high prices for seeds and medicines, including the communities from whom the biodiversity and knowledge first came.

If biopiracy continues, the poor will have to buy the very conditions of life which today are available for free from biodiversity. The list of biopiracy patents increases each year: from Latin America, the ayahuasca used by Amazonian healers as a hallucinogenic, the quinoia, yellow beans; from Africa, the yellow yam, serendipity berries, brazzein, endod, thaumatur; from India, neem, turmeric, pepper, basmati rice, ginger, bitter gourd.

Enslaving the Free Tree

By associating creativity only with capital, and denying creativity where people live outside the global market economy, the patenting of life allows the piracy of indigenous knowledge. The patenting of neem and basmati are examples of biopiracy. Neem, whose scientific name *Azadirichta indica* is derived from its Persian name, which means Free Tree, has been used for centuries in India as a medicine and as a pest-control agent. And for centuries the Western world ignored the neem tree and its properties – the practices of Indian peasants and doctors were not deemed worthy of attention by the majority of British, French and Portuguese colonists.

In the last few years, however, growing opposition to chemical products in the West, in particular to pesticides, has led to a sudden enthusiasm for the pharmaceutical properties of neem. Since 1985, over a dozen US patents have been taken out by US and Japanese firms on formulae for stable neem-based solutions and emulsions, and even for a neem-based toothpaste. At least four of these are owned by W. R. Grace of the USA, three by another US company, the Native Plant Institute; and two by the Japanese Terumo Corporation. Having garnered their patents and with the prospect of a licence from the Environmental Protection Agency (EPA), W. R. Grace have set about manufacturing and commercializing their product by establishing a base in India. The company approached several Indian manufacturers with proposals to buy up their technology or to convince them to stop producing value-added products and instead to supply the company with raw material. Grace is likely to be followed by other patent-holding companies. 'Squeezing bucks out of the neem ought to be relatively easy,' observes *Science* magazine.

W. R. Grace's justification for patents pivots on the claim that these modernized extraction processes constitute a genuine innovation: 'Although traditional knowledge inspired the research and development that led to these patented composition and processes, they were considered sufficiently novel and different from the original product of nature and the traditional method of use to be patentable.'

In short, the processes are supposedly novel and an advance on Indian techniques. However, this novelty exists mainly in the context of the ignorance of the West. Over the 2000 years that neem-based biopesticides and medicines have been used in India, many complex processes were developed to make them available for specific use, though the active ingredients were not given Latinized scientific names. Common knowledge and common use of neem was one of the primary reasons given by the Indian Central Insecticide Board for not registering neem products under the Insecticides Act, 1968. The Board argued that neem materials had been in extensive use in India for various purposes since time immemorial, without any known deleterious effects.

We at the Research Foundation for Science, Technology and Ecology (RFSTE) in India, the International Federation of Organic Agriculture Movements (IFOAM) and also the European Greens challenged the neem patent No. 0436257 B1, jointly held by the US government and W. R. Grace, in the European Patent Office on grounds of piracy. On 10 May 2000, on the basis of our challenge, the USDA and W. R. Grace neem patent was revoked. The EPO stated categorically that this patent was based on the piracy of existing knowledge systems and lacked novelty and inventiveness. We succeeded in liberating the Free Tree as one step in the fight against biopiracy.

Stealing the Aroma of Basmati

The patenting of basmati is another example of blatant biopiracy. Basmati, is one of the distinct 200,000 varieties of rice evolved by Indian peasants. It is unique among the rices for its aroma, flavour, and long grain. Basmati, the Sanskrit name for this naturally perfumed rice, means 'ingrained aroma' or 'queen of aroma'. Basmati has been grown for centuries in the subcontinent as is evident from references in ancient texts, folklore and poetry. One of the earliest references to basmati according to the CSS Haryana Agricultural University, Hissar, is made in the famous epic of *Heer Ranjha*, written by the poet Varis Shah in 1766. This rice has always been treasured and possessively guarded by nobles, and coveted by foreigners.

Years of research on basmati strains by Indian and Pakistani farmers, has resulted in a wide range of basmati varieties. The superior qualities of this rice must be recognized as predominantly the contributions of the farmers' innovation. There are 27 distinct documented varieties of basmati grown in India. Basmati covers 10–15 per cent of the total land area under rice cultivation in India, and 650,000 tonnes of basmati are grown annually. Non-basmati and basmati rice is exported to more than eighty countries across the world. Between 400,000 to 500,000 tonnes of basmati are exported annually, and it has been one of the fastest growing export items from India in recent years. The main importers are the Middle East (65 per cent of basmati exports), Europe (20 per cent) and USA (10–15 per cent). Indian basmati exports to the EU in 1996–97 amounted to nearly 100,000 tonnes. At $850 a tonne, Indian basmati rice is the most expensive rice imported by the European Union, compared to $700 a tonne for Pakistani basmati and $500 a tonne for Thai fragrant rice (RFSTE, *Basmati Biopiracy*, 1998).

On 2 September 1997, the Texas-based RiceTec Inc. was granted Patent No. 5663484 on basmati rice lines and grains. At this time the company was already trading in rice with its own brand names, such as Kasmati, Texmati and Jasmati. This patent will allow RiceTec Inc. to sell a 'new' variety of basmati, which the company claims to have developed under the name of Basmati, in the United States of America and abroad. The following abstract from the patent, issued by the US Patent and Trademark Office (USPTO) demonstrates what a broad patent it is:

> The invention relates to novel rice lines and to plants and grains of these lines and to a method for breeding these lines. The invention also relates to a novel means for determining the cooking and starch properties of rice grains and its use in identifying desirable rice lines. Specifically, one aspect of the invention relates to novel rice lines whose plants are semi-dwarf in stature, substantially photo period insensitive and high-yielding, and produce rice grains having characteristics similar or superior to those of good quality Basmati produced for novel rice lines. The invention provides a method for breeding these novel rice lines.

A patent is granted for an industrial invention which is novel in a non-obvious way. The aroma of basmati rice is not novel. It has existed for centuries. It is a gift of nature which has been developed by the farmers of India and Pakistan. The variety for which RiceTec has claimed a patent has been derived from Indian basmati crossed with semi-dwarf varieties including *indica* varieties. Crossing different varieties to mix traits is a very common method known to everyone familiar with the art of breeding. In fact, the Indian national agricultural system has released new semi-dwarf varieties, Kasturi and Pusa Basmati-1. The RiceTec patent application states that these 'new varieties more properly should be described as basmati substitute or quasi-basmati'. However, it claims 'characteristics and qualities similar or superior to those of good quality basmati rice grains produced in India and Pakistan'.

Although the invention is described in detail with reference to specific embodiments thereof, it will be understood that variations which are functionally equivalent are within the scope of this invention. Indeed, various modifications of the invention in addition to those shown and described herein will become apparent to those skilled in the art from the foregoing description and accompanying drawings. Such modifications are extended to fall within the scope of the appended claims.

Although the patent is for a particular variety of basmati rice, the clause 'functional equivalents' in the claim has widespread implications. If the patent claim is interpreted to apply to all *functional varieties* of basmati which were used to develop the patented variety (Basmati 867), Indian and Pakistani farmers could be forced to pay royalties to RiceTec Inc. for the use of their own seeds and strains. The livelihood of 250,000 farmers growing basmati could be jeopardized.

A patent can only be issued if it meets the three criteria of novelty, non-obviousness and utility. Novelty implies that it must be new – it must not be part of 'prior art' or existing knowledge. Non-obviousness implies that someone familiar with the skills should not be able to achieve the same step. The development of the 'new' variety (Basmati 867) by RiceTec has been derived from Indian basmati through conventional breeding techniques. The claims of 'novelty' and 'invention' are therefore questionable.

Patents on indigenous knowledge rob the poor of their knowledge and skills – their capacity to meet their needs at zero or low cost from their local biodiversity. For corporations like Grace, RiceTec and Monsanto, the conversion of biology and indigenous knowledge into a global commodity is a source of limitless profits. For the Third World poor, the appropriation of their biological wealth and knowledge is a source of new poverty and new destitution. If the poor had to pay royalties for every seed they plant and every herbal medicine they prepare, they could not survive.

As seed and pesticide costs spiral with the market controlled by global corporations, poor peasants are pushed into debt, and even into suicide – 500 in India in the district of Warangal in Andhra Pradesh alone in 1998. The alternative of low-cost, internal-input and sustainable agriculture exists. However, because this does not generate billions of dollars of profits for the global 'life industry', it is ignored and marginalized.

The market expansion of capital into life's foundations and processes has to stop. Life must give rise to life, not profits. The restructuring of life for corporate control is violating the very basis of ecology and democracy.

Knowledge for Commerce or Survival

Knowledge in the Earth Family paradigm is based on ecology – it is evolved collectively and is freely shared to improve the wellbeing of all life, including human life. When biodiversity is reduced to a genetic mine, knowledge itself is mined through biopiracy, and is commodified and privatized. Sharing and exchange is criminalized and defined as 'intellectual property theft'. These two paradigms are in intense conflict in global trade and environment treaties.

The privatization of life and the reduction of living diversity and its parts and processes to tradeable commodities have been made legal obligations under the new free-trade arrangements of WTO – the institution established to implement the Uruguay Round of GATT. WTO has become a global constitution based on the logic and primacy of trade and commerce. The right to trade without limits, without barriers has been elevated to the supreme right. The right to protect living resources, livelihoods and lifestyles has been reduced to a 'barrier to free trade'.

Nonetheless, the right and obligation to protect life's diversity and diverse lifestyles is also an international, legally binding agreement that was signed at the Earth Summit in Rio in 1992. The treaty for the conservation of biodiversity, the Convention on Biological Diversity (CBD), makes the conservation and sustainable use of living resources an international obligation.

WTO, the global treaty for commerce, is in direct conflict with the 1992 Rio Convention on Biological Diversity, the global treaty for conservation. WTO requires the privatization of life through enforcing patents on life. CBD requires the protection of biological and cultural diversity. WTO undermines national sovereignty while CBD upholds the principle of national sovereignty. Under CBD, each state regulates access to its genetic resources and can deny it if it appears harmful to its national interests.

Under Article 3, CBD recognizes the sovereign rights that states have in accordance with the Charter of the United Nations

> ...to exploit their own resources pursuant to their own environmental policies, and the responsibility to ensure that activities within their jurisdiction or control do not cause damage to the environment of other States or of areas beyond the limits of national jurisdiction.

Article 8(j) recognizes that each state should:

> ...subject to its national legislation, respect, preserve and maintain the knowledge, innovations and practices of indigenous and local communities embodying traditional lifestyles relevant for the conservation and sustainable use of biological diversity and promote their wider application with the approval and involvement of the holders of such knowledge, innovations and practices and encourage the equitable sharing of the benefits arising from the utilization of such knowledge, innovation and practices.

CBD acknowledges the role of local farmers and tribals in bio-conservation, and obliges states to provide avenues for the protection of farmers' and national rights to biodiversity, and indigenous knowledge. Furthermore, it exhorts states to protect and encourage customary use of biological resources in accordance with cultural and traditional practices that are compatible with conservation or sustainable use requirements. Articles 10(a) and 10(c) directs the contracting parties to: 'Integrate consideration of the conservation and sustainable use of biological resources into national decision making and protect and encourage customary use of biological resources in accordance with traditional cultural practices that are compatible with conservation or sustainable use requirements. In accordance with Article 10 (c): 'Contracting parties are obliged to protect and encourage customary use of biological resources in accordance with traditional cultural practices to conserve and sustainably use these resources.'

WTO in effect protects the commercial rights of global corporations wanting to profit from trade in genes, cells, plants, seeds, animals and their manipulation through patents. Since these commercial rights are in conflict with the right of all species and all peoples to survival, WTO calls into question the sanctity of life and undermines the CBD. The global corporations that today have reconstituted themselves as life-sciences corporations have admitted that they drafted the TRIPs Agreement of the WTO which gives them the right to own and control living resources. As a representative of Monsanto has stated, 'We were the physician, the diagnostician, the patient – all in one.'

The conflict between knowledge for profits and knowledge for sustenance, between commerce and conservation makes it impossible for countries to take care of life forms that are rapidly being eroded and driven to extinction. Further, while birds and butterflies have no lobbies to push for laws for conservation, the life industry is highly organized and is pushing countries to introduce laws for patenting seeds and living resources on the one hand, and on the other preventing countries from passing laws to regulate genetic engineering and its products.

India was taken by the USA to the WTO dispute settlement mechanism for not implementing TRIPs fast enough, though it was the democratic debates in the Indian parliament that caused the delay. The WTO ruled against India, and India is now being forced to grant patents in the area of medicine and agrichemicals. Since many patents related to living resources are based on biopiracy, i.e. the patenting of indigenous knowledge, the WTO is in fact forcing India to enclose its biological and intellectual commons.

This is the reason for the worldwide outrage against the corporate rights to monopolize life enshrined in the TRIPs agreement of WTO. Since these agreements are to be reviewed in the year 2000, some countries, including India and the African states, are calling for a change in IPR regimes to prevent patents on life and biopiracy, and a resolution of the conflict between commerce and conservation, and between WTO and CBD. Meantime, civil society movements are working to retain the sanctity and sovereignty of life from the colonizing and monopolizing control of global corporations. Living democracy is about the protection and maintenance of the Earth Family.

The Movement to Stop Biopiracy

When TRIPs was forced on countries during the Uruguay Round of GATT in 1995, many issues of public concern were totally bypassed, and the full ethical, ecological and economic implications of patenting life were not discussed. Third World countries were coerced into accepting that Western-style IPR systems were 'strong' and 'advanced'. However, public-interest groups showed that these systems were strong in establishing corporate monopolies globally, but weak in protecting indigenous knowledge and preventing biopiracy. They were an 'advanced' means for taking away the resources of the poor, and stealing the knowledge of our grand-mothers, but primitive when viewed from the perspective of justice, equality and cross-cultural respect.

As a result of sustained public pressure, after the agreement came into force in 1995 many Third World countries made recommendations for changes in Article 27.3 (b) to prevent biopiracy. India in its discussion paper submitted to the TRIPs Council stated:

> Patenting of life forms may have at least two dimensions. Firstly, there is the ethical question of the extent of private ownership that could be extended to life forms. The second dimension relates to the use of IPRs' concept as understood in the industrialized world and its appropriateness in the face of the larger dimension of rights on knowledge, their ownership, use, transfer and dissemination. Informal systems, e.g. the *shrutis* and *smritis* in the Indian tradition

and grandmother's potions all over the world get scant recognition. To create systems that fail to address this issue can have severe adverse consequences on mankind, some say even leading to extinction.

Clearly there is a case for re-examining the need to grant patents on life forms anywhere in the world. Meanwhile, it may be advisable to:

1 Exclude patents on all life forms.

2 If (1) is not possible then exclude patents based on traditional/indigenous knowledge and essentially derived patents based on traditional/ indigenous knowledge and essentially derived products and processes from such knowledge

3 Or at least insist on the disclosure of the country of origin of the biological source and associated knowledge, and obtain the consent of the country providing the resource and knowledge, to ensure an equitable sharing of benefits.

Bolivia, Columbia, Ecuador, Nicaragua and Peru made a proposal entitled the Protection of the Intellectual Property Rights Relating to the Traditional Knowledge of Local and Indigenous Communities. This states: 'The entire modern evolution of intellectual property has been framed by principles and systems which have tended to leave aside a large sector of human creativity, namely the traditional knowledge possessed by local and indigenous communities.' The group proposed that negotiations be initiated at the ministerial conference in Seattle in November 1999, with a view to establishing a multilateral legal framework that will grant effective protection to the expressions and manifestations of traditional knowledge.

The African group has also called for systems to protect traditional knowledge and proposed that a footnote should be added to Article 27.3 (b) stating that any *sui generis* (self-standing) law for the protection of plant variety can provide for the protection of the innovations of indigenous and local farming communities in developing countries, consistent with CBD and the International Undertaking on Plant Genetic Resources.

In spite of the whole African group, five countries in Central and Latin America and India calling for changes in 27.3 (b) on the basis of their right to a review as built into the agreement, the USA and Europe are determined to block the reform of TRIPs and any attempt to stop biopiracy. In a 'Green Room' consultation (the undemocratic structure of decision-making in WTO) the powerful industrialized countries told Mike Moore, the Director General, that they rejected all the proposals for the reform of TRIPs.

In preparation for the Seattle talks in November 1999, the African group and India also called for the exclusion of life forms from patentability, and for the WTO to be subordinate to CBD. The USA and Europe rejected the developing countries' proposals related to 27.3 (b) on the grounds that the WTO cannot be subordinated to other international agreements, which confirms the belief of the environment movement that in WTO issues of environment are always sacrificed for trade.

Using WTO, the rich North is committed to protecting corporate monopoly rights at any cost, even if this means undermining protections for nature and people guaranteed by international agreements and national constitutions. In its submission related to the TRIPs review, the USA has stated categorically that it 'believes that an exception to patentability, authorized by Article 27.3 (b) is unnecessary and, therefore, treats plants and animals and non-biological and microbiological processes as patentable subject matter under its law'.

The USA heralded the beginning of patents on life with the Chakrabarty patent on a genetically engineered microorganism as 'extremely fortuitous'. In granting the first patent on life in 1980, the US Supreme Court interpreted life as 'manufacture' and 'constitution of matter'. Reducing complex living systems to a machine and mere constitution of matter allowed industrial patents to be applied to life forms, since the distinctiveness of living organisms had been defined away. This made possible the patenting of seeds, cows, sheep, human cells and microorganisms. As the US paper on the TRIPs review states, 'The Supreme Court's decision in Diamond, Commissioner of Patents and Trademarks vs Chakrabarty spurred the development of a new industry – the biotechnology industry.' The USA is, therefore, committed to patents on life in order to defend its biotech industry. But having opened the floodgates to treating life forms and these modifications as patentable, the US patent office started to grant patents not just to GMOs (genetically modified organisms) but to processes and products derived from biodiversity using indigenous knowledge. This is how US patents on neem, karela, turmeric and basmati have been granted.

On the issue of biopiracy, the USA states that the requirement that patent applicants identify in their application the source of any genetic materials or traditional knowledge used in developing their claim 'would be impractical'. Recognizing and screening indigenous knowledge should be a necessary element of the test for inventiveness and novelty that is required under any patent system. However, when it comes to the traditional knowledge of the Third World, this screening for 'prior art' is declared impractical. Forcing all countries to change their patent laws in spite of protests is considered practical. Imposing patents on life in spite of the fact that people in the North and South do not accept patents on life is considered practical. Enforcing property rights on seed is considered practical. Collecting royalties from the poor in the Third World for resources and knowledge that came from them in the first place is considered practical. But taking the simple step of changing one clause in one law in the USA and one clause in TRIPs is considered impractical, although it could go a long way to countering biopiracy.

The USA proposes that the Third World should solve the problem of biopiracy by granting access to the companies that are patenting indigenous knowledge: 'The most effective means for exercising these rights would appear to be to require that parties seeking access to genetic resources or traditional knowledge enter into a contract with the sovereign entity that grants that access.' (US submission to WTO). Instead of correcting the deficiencies in TRIPs and US-style patent laws, the USA would like to maintain the structures and laws that permit biopiracy at a global level. The USA suggests that the Third World write contracts with the biopirates. This is as if the police were to ask a person whose house has been burgled to make a deal with the burglar instead of arresting the culprit.

Citizens of the world will not let this go unchallenged. That is why in Seattle in November 1999 citizens' groups launched a Global Campaign Against Biopiracy to ensure that TRIPs and US laws are changed, and that Third World countries can take steps to protect their rich biological and intellectual heritage, and the poor of the world are not denied their basic human rights to food and health.

CHAPTER 2

GENETIC MODIFICATION AND FRANKENSTEIN FOODS

For 10,000 years agriculture has been based on the strategy of conserving and enhancing genetic diversity. Humans have all this time domesticated and modified wild plants and animals, the gifts of nature's biodiversity. According to Erna Bennett (former genetic resources expert to the Food and Agricultural Organization of the UN), 'The patchwork of cultivation sown by man unleashed an explosion of literally inestimable numbers of new races of cultivated plants and their relatives.' (Hawkes, *Conservation and Agriculture*, 1978.)

Prior to planting crops, humans harvested wild plants. For example, corn, rice and wheat were originally collected from the wild. For gathering societies, less than a month of harvesting from the wild could ensure enough for the year's needs. For reasons unknown to us, human societies moved from harvesting wild grain to domesticating and sowing the seeds of those grains. This is a process that still continues. A farmer participating in the Indian Seed-Saving Movement, Navdanya, which is dedicated to conserving native biodiversity, domesticated a wild rice in 1998.

Domestication changed the nature of plants. As Cary Fowler and Pat Mooney have described in their book *Shattering* (1990):

The simple act of harvesting seeds of non-domesticated plants and then sowing them produced remarkable changes of great advantage to people. Weeds and grass, as everyone knows, are extraordinarily adept at spreading their seeds. The survival of such plants depends on their ability to spread their seeds.... The unavoidable collection of non-shattering types caused the first fields planted by the first farmers to be constituted primarily of grasses significantly different in one respect from those that grow wild. Repeated sowings of these seeds produced non-shattering plants – plants whose seed or grain would remain on the plant even if jostled by the emerging farmer with a flint-bladed sickle. Genetically, the change was simple. Often the difference between shattering and non-shattering types is caused by just one or two genes, the biological carriers of heredity. With non-shattering grains, people were able to harvest a greater percentage of all the seeds in the field. Harvested yield increased, giving these first farmers positive response for their efforts.

Farmers selected, improved, evolved crops and seeds over the centuries, and created the tremendous diversity of crops and cultures that have nourished the world. Crops were bred for local ecological conditions – for resistance to drought or to waterlogging, for surviving salinity or frost. The first-generation plants bred for domestication were based on farmers' knowledge, on the principle of diversity, and on working with nature.

The Green Revolution

The second generation of plants bred for agriculture came to be known as the Green Revolution. The crossbreeding of different varieties to make them more resistant to chemicals was a departure from the earlier centuries of plant breeding based on farmers' knowledge. Firstly, the farmer was displaced by professional breeders. Secondly, ecological processes of food production were replaced by ecologically destructive methods, such as intensive use of water and of synthetic chemicals. Industrial breeding also destroyed the genetic diversity of crops as monocultures of industrially bred seed spread worldwide into ecosystems for which they were not adapted. Linked to the centralized strategy for breeding 'voracious varieties' of seeds (those that consume high levels of fertilizers and water) was the need for uniformity and the destruction of diversity. Uniformity became imperative from the view of centralized production of seeds as well as centralized provision of inputs like water and fertilizers.

Released in Japan in 1935, a wheat known as Norin was a cross between a Japanese dwarf wheat and an American wheat that the Japanese government had imported from the USA in 1887. Norin was brought to US in 1946 by Dr D. C. Salmon, an agriculturist acting as a US military adviser in Japan, and further crossed with an American variety by US Department of Agriculture scientist Dr Orville Vogel. Vogel sent the strain in the 1950s to CIMMYT, the international maize and wheat centre in Mexico. There it was used by Norman Borlaug, who was on the Rockefeller Foundation staff, in nine years of experimenting, to develop his well known Mexican varieties. Of the thousands of dwarf seeds created by Borlaug, only three went on to create the Green Revolution wheat plants that were spread worldwide. On this narrow and alien genetic base the food supplies of millions are precariously perched.

Global rice monocultures were created by sending seeds across the world from the International Rice Research Institute (IRRI). The first release, IR-8, was a cross between the Indonesian variety and a dwarf strain from Taiwan. The various IR-varieties were prone to pests and diseases owing to monocropping and a narrow genetic base, which meant that in turn more toxic pesticides would be required. This environmental cost was justified on the grounds of increasing food production.

The new seeds were called high-yielding varieties, or miracle varieties that would make possible the end of hunger and famine. However, the dwarf gene was essential to the technological package of the Green Revolution, which was based on intensive inputs of chemical fertilizers. The taller traditional varieties tended to convert the fertilizers into overall plant growth, whereas the shorter, stiffer stems of dwarf varieties allowed more efficient conversion of nutrient into grain. The connection between chemical fertilizers and dwarf varieties that were established through the breeding programmes of CIMMYT and IRRI, created a major shift in how seeds were perceived and produced, and in who controlled the production and use of seeds.

The Green Revolution varieties were not intrinsically higher yielding than the farmers' varieties that they displaced, nor did the industrial monocultures provide more food than diversified, ecologically managed small farms. In a 15-nation study of the impact of the seeds (UN Research Institute for Social Development), D. Palmer concluded that the term 'high-yielding varieties' (HYVs) is a misnomer since it implies that the new seeds are high-yielding in themselves. Their distinguishing feature is, in fact, that they are highly responsive to certain key inputs such as fertilizers and irrigation. Palmer therefore suggested the term 'high-responsive varieties', HRVs, in place of HYVs (quoted in Lappé and Collins, *Food First*, 1982). The gain in yield is insignificant compared to the increase in inputs.

The measurement of output is also biased by restricting it to the marketable part of crops, and to the yield of individual crops. Food is necessary not only for people. Ensuring adequate organic matter to feed animals and the soil is essential for sustainable agriculture. In dwarf varieties grain is increased at the expense of straw production, so output is affected in two dimensions – food is diverted from other species, and ecological cycles that maintain soil fertility and food production for the future are also destroyed.

Gene Transfer and Jumping Genes

Genetic engineering in agriculture has often been called the second Green Revolution. Genetic engineering does in fact accelerate the Green Revolution trends towards the spread of chemicals, the expansion of monocultures and the destruction of agrobiodiversity, but in addition creates risks of genetic pollution or biopollution.

While it is true that humans have been modifying plants from the beginning of agriculture, it is not true that all modifications are ecologically equivalent and have similar impact. Modifications introduced by farmers were different from those of the industrial breeders of Green Revolution varieties. The former increased biodiversity, the latter reduced it.

The modifications introduced by genetic engineers are different again. These organisms result from mixing species that would not normally mix in nature. New ecological risks arise from the possibilities of moving genes across organisms to create 'transgenic' organisms. The ecological structure, function and impact of these novel organisms on other species, on the environment and on human health is therefore different from wild or conventionally bred relatives.

Genes are functional units formed by sequences of a molecule called DNA (deoxyribose nucleic acid) and are considered the unit of heredity in all living organisms. The structure of DNA was first identified by James Watson and Francis Crick who showed it to be a double helix. Strings of DNA are called chromosomes. All living organisms are made of cells, and each cell has a nucleus in which strings of DNA are organized as chromosomes. When fertilization occurs in animals or plants, there are two sets of chromosomes that pair in the embryonic cell – one inherited from the female parent, the other from the male. The cells formed on fertilization continue to divide and multiply, and the genetic material in each new cell is identical.

There are two paradigms of the role and function of genes in living organisms – the reductionist and the non-reductionist. According to the reductionist paradigm, genes are the blueprint of life, the master molecule that determines the structure and function of living organisms. In this paradigm, genes act independently of other genes, the rest of the organism and the environment.

As non-reductionist biologists stress, however, genes act in context, and in relationship to other parts of the organisms and to other organisms and the environment. Crick and Watson explained how DNA can encode information, replicate and mutate. However, to leap from the local functions of genes defined by individual proteins to complex functions of living organisms is unjustified. This extended theory of the gene as the basis of life is being questioned by leading biologists who take the ecology of the gene and the ecology of the organism into account. Unfortunately, precisely at the time when scientists are questioning genetic reductionism, reductionism is becoming the basis of the new biotechnologies, the new life sciences industry and the new genetic commerce. Genetic engineering allows DNA to be moved across species boundaries, with the idea of introducing particular traits. As Brian Goodwin, one of the world's leading theoretical biologists makes clear:

> The assumption is that a characteristic can be transferred from one species to another simply by moving the gene. The problem is that

genes are defined by context. For example, a gene that in a mouse produces a hormone regulating growth will have one effect in the mouse, but the same gene producing the hormone in a human being will have a very different effect. So as we move genes from one species to another, we will keep getting unpredictable effects which simply could not have been anticipated.

(Quoted in Suzuki, *From Naked Ape to Super Species*, 1999)

In spite of the growth of theoretical insights and empirical evidence supporting the non-reductionist approach to genes, genetic determinism is still powerful – mechanistic paradigms have been the legacy of the first Industrial Revolution, and reductionism serves industry well. Reductionist biologists have gone far in raising the gene above the organism and demoting the organism itself to a mere machine. The purpose, the sole purpose of this machine is its own survival and reproduction, or perhaps to put it more accurately, the survival and reproduction of the DNA that is said both to programme and to 'dictate' its operation. In Richard Dawkins's terms, an organism is a 'survival machine' – a 'lumbering robot' constructed to house genes, those 'engines of self-preservation' that have as their primary property inherent 'selfishness'. They are sealed off from the outside world, communicating with it by tortuous indirect routes, manipulating it by remote control. They are in you and in me; they created us, body and mind; and their preservation is the ultimate rationale for our existence (Dawkins, *The Selfish Gene*, 1976).

In the mechanistic, reductionist model, the building blocks are atoms or substances or matter. Genes have no internal relations. They are the nuts and bolts that make a machine. Nuts and bolts cannot evolve, they can merely be rearranged. In biology the mechanistic model has taken genes to be the atoms that constitute living systems. In this billiard-ball model, the genes are assumed to be particles located on chromosomes. The genes make proteins, proteins make us, and the genes replicate themselves. In 1926, in *The Gene as the Basis of Life*, biologist H. J. Muller wrote that the gene can be viewed as a biological atom, solely responsible for the physiological and morphological properties of life forms (see Keller, *A Feeling for the Organism*, 1983).

Reductionism was promoted strongly by the biologist August Weismann, who nearly a century ago postulated the complete separation of the reproductive cells – the germ line – from the functional body, or soma. According to Weismann, reproductive cells are already set apart in the early embryo, and they continue their segregated existence into maturity, when they contribute to the formation of the next generation. This supported the non-heritability of acquired traits with no direct feedback from environment to heredity.

The reductionist assumption that genes are 'atoms' of life and determinants of properties of life forms is linked to the assumption that information only flows in one direction from genes to organisms. This genetic determinism was reinforced by the emergence of molecular biology and the discovery in the 1950s of the role of nucleic acid. Molecular biology showed a means of transferral of information from genes to proteins, but gave no indication, until recently, of any transfer in the opposite direction. The inference that there could be none became what Crick called the 'central dogma' of molecular biology: 'Once information has passed into proteins, it cannot get out again.'

Isolating the gene as a 'master molecule' is part of biological determinism. The 'central dogma' that genes as DNA make proteins is another aspect of this determinism. This dogma is preserved even though it is known that genes 'make' nothing and that the complex living organism in complex relationship with the environment is what 'makes' living systems.

The non-reductionist view of genes and living systems locates genes in the ecological complexity of organisms. As Richard Lewontin, the molecular biologist has stated:

> DNA is a dead molecule, among the most non-reactive, chemically inert molecules in the world. It has no power to reproduce itself. Rather, it is produced out of elementary materials by a complex cellular machinery of proteins. While it is often said that DNA produces proteins, in fact proteins (enzymes) produce DNA. When we refer to genes as self-

replicating, we endow them with a mysterious autonomous power that seems to place them above the more ordinary materials of the body.
Yet if anything in the world can be said to be self-replicating, it is not the gene, but the entire organism as a complex system.

(*The Doctrine of DNA*, 1993)

According to biologist Mae-Wan Ho in *Genetic Engineering: Dream or Nightmare?* (1997), there are three assumptions of the reductionist paradigm:

- Genes determine character in a straightforward additive.
- Genes and genomes are stable, and except for rare random mutations, are passed on unchanged to the next generation.
- Genes and genomes cannot be changed directly in response to the environment.

None of these assumptions is true. Genes code for the thousands of metabolic reactions that provide the energy to do everything that constitutes being alive. These metabolic reactions form an immensely complicated network in which the product of our enzyme is processed by one or more other enzymes. Thus, no enzyme (or gene) ever works in isolation. Consequently, the same gene will have different effects from individual to individual because the other genes are different. The complicated network of interactive processes that connects different subsystems of a living organism is the real source of determining traits and properties of plants and animals.

This intricate network also responds to the environment. Barbara McClintock, who won the Nobel Prize in 1983 for her work on jumping genes, is of the opinion that, 'The functioning of genes is totally dependent on the environment in which they find themselves.' The term 'jumping genes' indicates that genomes are not stable but fluid and dynamic. Genes are not isolated atoms, unchanging and immutable, but flexible and interactive, and their behaviour is influenced by the larger networks within the genome and by the larger environment. But although the reductionist paradigm has given way to the non-reductionist paradigm in basic research, reductionism still guides genetic engineering.

What is Genetic Engineering?

Genetic engineering is the set of techniques, also referred to as recombinant (rDNA) technology, which is used for modifying and recombining genes from different organisms that would not naturally interbreed. Examples of transgenic organisms are:

- The introduction of flounder genes into strawberries for longer storage and larger travel distances on the assumption that the gene that allows flounders to survive in icy cold water would preserve strawberries.
- The introduction of hamster genes into tobacco to increase sterol production (which enhances the effect of the nicotine).
- The insertion of spider genes into goats to enable them to produce silk in their milk.
- The insertion of human genes into sheep to produce 'human' proteins in their milk.
- The introduction of human sperm-producing genes into rats to produce 'rat-man sperm' to fertilize human eggs. (Dessee, 'Unnatural Selection', *Wild Duck Review*, Summer 1999)

There are two principal methods of transferring foreign genes into crop plants. The first is to use bacterial or viral vectors to carry genes into a plant's genome. The second is the direct transfer of DNA using gene guns or microprojectiles.

Introducing foreign genes through bacterial or viral infections involves a number of steps. The first is to make recombinant DNA in test tubes by using enzymes (catalysing proteins) isolated from microorganisms to cut and join together pieces of DNA from different organisms. The genes are multiplied and then transferred into plants through 'vectors', which are usually viruses or plasmids (the small circular DNA structure in bacteria). Once inside the cells, the vectors with the transgene became a permanent part of the organism. Transgenic organisms are organisms that have been 'infected' by transgenes using vectors. The most common vectors are combinations of natural genetic parasites and infective agents, including viruses that cause diseases in plants and animals, with their pathogenic functions 'crippled'. The vector used most widely is derived from a tumour-inducing plasmid carried by the soil bacterium *Agrobacterium tumefacieus.* These bacteria naturally infect over one hundred plant species, and genetic engineers make use of this quality. But the gene-transfer method using *Agrobacterium* is labour-intensive and is unsuitable for cereal crops, such as rice, wheat and maize, since it does not naturally infect their species

This limitation has been overcome by direct-transfer methods using particle bombardment through 'gene guns' or 'gene cannons'. These methods were developed independently by John Saiford and colleagues at Cornell, and Dennis McCake and colleagues at Agracetus Company, USA, now owned by Monsanto. In the Biological Ballistics or 'Biolistic' method evolved at Cornell, magnesium tungsten or gold particles are coated with DNA and literally blasted into plant cells using a gunpowder detonation in a particle gun. The particles carrying DNA are accelerated at high velocity, enter the cell wall, and transfer the DNA. The Dupont Company has exclusive rights to use Cornell's patented Biolistic Gene Gun for developing commercial transgenic crop seed (Nottingham, *Eat Your Genes,* 1998). Agracetus's (or Monsanto's) 'Accell' method uses electrical discharge to propel accelerated DNA-coated gold particles into plant material. In 1988 Agracetus (now owned by Monsanto) was the first company to transfer foreign genes into soya beans, and Monsanto's Roundup Ready soya beans were developed using the Agracetus technology.

Transgenic plants produced either by introducing foreign genes through vectors or through particle bombardment have a low rate of success. To separate plants that have incorporated the foreign gene from those that have not, antibiotic-resistance markers have to be used. Genetically engineered plant cells are then grown in a medium containing this antibiotic. Those that survive are the ones that have taken up the transgene with the antibiotic-resistant marker attached. These are then cultured and grown into mature plants.

No matter how the transgene is introduced, there is total lack of predictability about the exact location in the chromosome where the gene is inserted. The common argument that genetic engineering is precise and predictable is not true. It is in fact not 'engineering' at all. The theoretical biologist Stuart Newman, interviewed for *Wild Duck Review* (Summer, 1999), said, 'It is a hit or miss production of potentially useful monstrosities. Genetic engineering does not qualify for the status of a technology, and is in fact being commercialized prematurely.'

As Terje Traavik, a leading molecular biologist, states:

'Technology' is derived from the Greek term 'tekhne' which is connected to handicraft or arts. Our associations with the word include predictability, control, and reproductibility. The parts of genetic engineering that concerns construction of vectors are truly technology. But present time techniques for moving new genes into cells and organisms mean:

- No possibility to target the vector/transgene to specific sites within the recipient genomes. In practical terms this means that modifications performed with identical recipients and vector gene constructs under the same standardized conditions may result in highly different GMOs depending on where the transgenes become inserted.
- No control with changes in gene expression patterns for the inserted or the endogenous genes of the GMO.
- No control of whether the inserted transgene(s), or parts thereof, move within or from the recipient genome, or where transferred DNA sequences end up in the ecosystems.

In the light of this, it seems both pertinent and relevant to ask the question whether genetic engineering at its present level of development deserves the label 'technology' at all.

(Terje Traavik, 'An Orphan in Science', 1999.)

The promoters of genetic engineering state that genetic engineering is no different from conventional breeding, and hence poses no new health or ecological risks. They also argue that it is more precise and predictable than conventional breeding. But conventional breeding does not transfer genes from bacteria and animals to plants. It does not put fish genes into potatoes or scorpion genes into cabbage. It crosses rice with rice, and wheat with wheat. Genetic engineering differs from conventional breeding for the following reasons:

1 Unlike conventional breeding, genetic engineering recombines genetic material from different unrelated species which do not interbreed in nature and for which there is no, or very little, probability of natural progeny. This has unpredictable effects on the physiology, biochemistry and ecological functions of the transgene organisms.

2 New exotic genes are introduced into unpredictable locations in the genome, while conventional breeding shuffles different versions of the same genes whose genome structure has been given by evolution. Introduction of exotic genes in unpredictable ways can lead to unpredictable effects on the metabolism, physiology, and biochemistry of the recipient transgene organism.

3 Genetic engineering uses vectors which are derived from disease-causing viruses and plasmids. Since these vectors are designed to shuttle genes between a wide range of species, they have a wide host range, and can infect a wide range of plants and animals. Further, since vectors are constructed to overcome the recipient organisms' defence mechanisms against invasion by foreign DNA, genetic engineering carries the risk of reducing resistance and immunity and making plants more vulnerable to infections.

The Spread of GE Crops

The most significant spread of crops grown from genetically engineered seed is in the USA. Worldwide more than 28 million hectares (70 acres) have been planted with genetically engineered seed. Of this, 71 per cent is accounted for by herbicide-resistant soya bean, corn and cotton. Thousands of acres have also been planted with accidentally contaminated seeds.

The commercialized staple food crops that are genetically engineered are currently only three in number: soya bean, corn, canola. The trends in cultivation of transgenic crops show that genetic engineering is displacing the diverse foods that people of diverse cultures have used in their diets. Cropping systems for GMOs are based on expanding monocultures of the same variety evolved for single-function response. In 1996, 769,000 hectares (1.9 million acres) were planted with only two varieties of Bt. cotton (genetically engineered to produce the pest-killing toxin of the organism *Bacillus thuringiensis*) and 526,000 hectares (1.3 million acres) with the same Roundup Ready soya bean. As the biotechnology industry globalizes, these monoculture tendencies will increase, further displacing agricultural biodiversity and creating ecological vulnerability.

The Green Revolution narrowed the basis of food security by displacing diverse nutritious food grains and spreading monocultures of rice, wheat and maize, but it did focus on staple foods and their yields. The Genetic Engineering Revolution is undoing the narrow gains of the Green Revolution both by neglecting the diversity of staples and by not addressing the issue of yields. Yield increase does not even exist in the list of traits being introduced into transgenic crops. Fifty-four per cent of the increase in transgenic crops is accounted for by herbicide-resistance which implies increased use of herbicides, not increased food. As an industry briefing paper (James, 'Global Status of Transgenic Crops in 1997') accepts, 'The herbicide-tolerant gene has no effect on yield *per se.*'

There are two main justifications for the spread of genetic engineering in agriculture. The first is that it will increase yields and will contribute to food security. The second is that it will reduce the use of chemicals and will contribute to sustainable agriculture and the protection of the environment. However, both are without foundation. Genetic engineering will in fact increase food insecurity, not reduce it. It will also increase pollution, both by spreading the use of agrichemicals and by creating new risks of biopollution. Also used to promote GM foods is the myth of their safety on the grounds that they are 'substantially equivalent' to conventionally produced food. I challenge these three myths and aim to show that biotechnology in food and agriculture is characterized by the following realities: that genetic engineering, like the Green Revolution, will create hunger by destroying the livelihoods and resources of the poorest two-thirds of humanity; that genetic engineering poses a threat to the planet both by increasing chemical use and by destroying bio-diversity; that by the biotechnology industry itself, GMOs are claimed as 'novel' and hence *not* substantially equivalent to conventional crops. In addition, scientific evidence about the risks of genetic engineering is growing.

The Myth of Feeding the World

The biotechnology industry argues that no other technology can increase food production as efficiently as industrial breeding and biotechnology. However, this argument is flawed:

- Industrial breeding focuses on partial yields of single crops rather than total yields of multiple crops and integrated systems.
- Industrial breeding focuses on yields of one or two globally traded commodities, not on the diverse crops that people eat.
- Industrial breeding focuses on quantity per acre rather than on nutrition per acre.
- Industrial agriculture has very low productivity judged on the basis of resource use.
- Industrial agriculture undermines food security by using up resources that could have been used for sustainable food production.

A 1998 report on a study by the Rural Advancement Foundation International (RAFI) states:

Of some 320,000 vascular plants, about 3,000 species (both 'wild' and domesticated) are regularly exploited as food, while the total number of plant species cultivated and collected by humans exceeds 7,000. A recent study by Canadian researchers, Christine and Robert Prescott-Allen, used *per capita* food supply data from 146 countries and found that 103 species contribute 90 per cent of the world's plant food supply. However, thousands of species contribute to the food supply of the other 10 per cent which have considerable importance from a nutritional viewpoint and for poor people.

Ecological alternatives can increase food supply through biodiversity intensification instead of chemical intensification and genetic engineering, and this is discussed in Chapter 4.

The global trends of the growth of genetically engineered crops is seen in the table below. The commercialized staple food crops that are genetically engineered are currently only three in number. In place of hundreds of legumes and beans eaten around the world, there is only soya bean. In place of diverse varieties of millets, wheat and rice, there is only corn. In place of the diversity of oil seeds, there is only canola. The trends in cultivation of transgenic crops show that genetic engineering is displacing the diverse foods that people of diverse cultures have used in their diets. Its focus is on non-food commercial crops like tobacco and cotton and on crops like soya bean which before were not staples for most cultures outside East Asia. Transgenic tobacco, cotton, tomato are not food staples and will not feed the hungry. Food security has cultural dimensions, and soya will not provide food security for dal-eating Indians, nor corn for the sorghum belt of Africa.

TABLE 1

Global area of transgenic crops 1996–97
40% soya bean
25% corn
13% tobacco
11% cotton
10% canola
1% tomato
1% potato

The Myth of High Yields

Diverse farmers' varieties of food crops have been replaced by the supposed high-yielding varieties (HYVs). These HYVs have been bred only to yield enhanced grain production, that is, a high *partial* yield. They exhibit low *total system* yield. HYVs fail to produce enough straw that is adequate in quality or quantity to feed livestock or soils. The increase in marketable output of grain has been achieved at the cost of decrease of biomass for animals and soils and of the decrease of ecosystem productivity due to overuse of resources. Indigenous varieties outperform HYVs in *total system* yield. When the total biomass (grain plus straw) is taken into account, traditional farming systems based on indigenous varieties are not found to be low-yielding. In fact many native varieties have higher yields both in terms of grain output as well as of total biomass output than the supposed HYVs that have been introduced in their place.

While these reductionist categories of yield and productivity allow a higher measurement of yields, they exclude the measurement of the ecological destruction that affects future yields. Productivity in traditional farming practices has always been high if it is remembered that very little external inputs are required. While the Green Revolution has been projected as having increased productivity in the absolute sense, when resource-utilization is taken into account, it has been found to be counterproductive and resource-inefficient ('Starving the Four Billion and Destroying the Planet', RFSTE briefing paper for the Convention on Biodiversity, May 1997).

The increased yields from genetically engineered crops is the most important argument used by the genetic engineering industry. However, genetic engineering has actually led to decline in yields. Bill Christianson, a US soya bean farmer at the first conference on 'Biodevastation' at St Louis, Missouri, the headquarters of Monsanto, in July 1998, said that in Missouri, genetically engineered soya had a five bushel per acre decrease in yield. Ed Oplinger, Professor of Agronomy at the University of Wisconsin, has been carrying out yield trials on soya bean for 25 years. On the basis of data he collected in 12 states which grow 80 per cent of US soya, he found genetically engineered soya beans had 4 per cent lower yields than conventional varieties (Holzman, *Genetic Engineering News*, April 1999).

In a study by Marc Lappé and Britt Bailey, in 30 out of 38 varieties conventional soya beans outperformed the transgenic ones, with an overall drop in yield of 10 per cent compared to conventional varieties (*Against the Grain*, 1999). Dr Charles Benbrook reported a 6.7 per cent decline in yields in soya beans engineered for resistance to the herbicide Roundup on the basis of 8,200 university-based varietal trials in

1998. 'If not reversed by future breeding enhancements, this down-ward shift in soya bean yield potential could emerge as the most significant decline in major crop ever associated with a single genetic modification.' (Ag Biotech Info Net Technical Paper, 13 July 1999).

Rodney Garrison was among the US farmers who believed in Monsanto's miracle Roundup Ready cotton, a cotton variety resistant to the Monsanto herbicide Roundup. However, in the Mississippi delta where he farms, officials are warning farmers to hold off until further testing. Dozens of farmers are seeking millions of dollars in damages from Monsanto and its partner Delta-Pine arising from cotton boll damage in the 1997 Roundup Ready cotton harvest, perhaps caused by the genetic structure. Farmers have lost up to 40 per cent of their crop. The Mississippi Seed Arbitration Council ruled that Monsanto's Roundup Ready cotton failed to perform as adver-tised, and recommended payments of nearly $2 million to three cotton farmers who suffered severe losses.

Bacillus thuringiensis (Bt.) is a naturally occurring organism which produces a toxin. Genes for Bt. toxins are being added to a wide range of crops to enable the plants to produce their own insecticide. In the first trials of Bt. cotton undertaken in India, the yields were sometimes dramatically lower than that of non-Bt. cotton

The Myth of Decreased Chemical Use

In pushing genetic engineering, chemical corporations have used various strategies to make the public believe that biotechnology in agriculture implies the end of chemical hazards and that it 'protects the planet' (International Association of Plant Breeders, *Feeding the Eight Billion and Preserving the Planet*, 1998). But there are four reasons why biotechnology will lead to an increase in chemical use:

- The predominant application of genetic engineering in agriculture is in growing crops resistant to specific herbicides. This will increase rather than reduce herbicide use.
- The use of chemicals will spread to new regions of the world formerly free of intensive chemical use in agriculture.

- Applications, such as engineering Bt. toxin in plants, can actually lead to increased pesticide use through build up of Bt.-resistance and the destruction of ecological alternatives for pest control.
- The engineering of a toxin into the plant itself might increase toxins in the plant and in the ecosystem.

Roundup is a broad-spectrum herbicide that kills everything green. In the words of Monsanto's President:

Many of you have heard of Monsanto's Roundup herbicide. It's non-persistent...biodegrading within a few weeks after application. It doesn't leach into groundwater. It's essentially non-toxic to human and other animals. And it's very effective at killing weeds – so effective, in fact, that Roundup would control soyabeans as well as weeds if it should come into contact with both. At least, that was the case until Monsanto developed Roundup Ready soya beans. Roundup Ready soya beans express a novel protein which allows them to thrive, even when sprayed with enough Roundup to control competing weed. With the spread of Roundup through genetically engineered crops, Monsanto has requested and received permission for a threefold increase in herbicide residues on genetically engineered soyabeans. They can now sell soyabeans contaminated with 20 parts per million compared to the earlier unit of 6 parts per million.

Glyphosate, the principal constituent of Roundup herbicide, can kill fish in concentrations of 10 parts per million. It kills earthworms, and is also toxic to many soil microorganisms that are essential for plant growth.

The use of Roundup resistant crops is forcing others to shift to genetically engineered crops because of pesticide drift. As Dr Ford Baldwin, a weed scientist from the University of Kansas, has reported, 'Pesticide-drift-caused crop destruction increases the pressure for non-users...to get on the Roundup Ready band wagon. A neighbouring farmer not using the technology stands to have his fields destroyed if the Roundup herbicide drifts on to his fields.'

Roundup Ready Soya (RRS) is the most widespread genetically engineered crop introduced so far. RRS is basically one of the strategies used to push sales of Monsanto's herbicide through its life-sciences division, which, as a PR exercise, is separated from the chemical division, but which is still involved in selling chemicals. Roundup accounts for 95 per cent of all sales of glyphosate, the world's best selling total herbicide, and in 1994 represented about 60 per cent of global non-selective herbicide sales. It is Monsanto's biggest selling product, and accounts for 17 per cent of total annual sales.

The second strategy to increase sales of Roundup is to spread the herbicide to countries where it has not been used before. In an adver-tising campaign in Europe in 1998, Monsanto claimed that its genetically engineered crops reduce pesticide use, and provide a safe and sustainable method of weed control. One of the ads stated: 'More biotechnology plants means less industrial ones.' However, while Monsanto was selling its Roundup Ready crops, it was also setting up new Roundup factories around the world. Monsanto has greatly increased its manufacturing capacity of glyphosate, investing US $200 million in production and formulation technology in Australia, Brazil, Belgium, India and China.

Herbicide-resistant crops are designed to be resistant to the propri-etary herbicides of the company, which makes money selling both seeds and chemicals. Monsanto requires farmers buying its Roundup resistant crops to sign a contract stating that that they will not buy chemicals from any other company and will not save seed. Monsanto has thus retained its monopoly through genetic engineering at a time (in the year 2000) when its patent for Roundup was expiring.

In biodiversity-rich regions, the spread of herbicide-resistant seeds will introduce toxic chemicals. These will destroy species as well as the livelihoods of the poorest, especially in those regions of the world where farms are small, labour is abundant, polycultures control weeds and women use the weeds for food and fodder – weeds form part of the rich biodiversity of small farms, and are a useful resource. Farming systems in the Third World depend on 100–200 plant species. Monsanto's Roundup advertisements in remote villages of

India state, 'Are your hands tied up by weeds? Roundup will set you free.' Yet one of the main purposes of Roundup Ready crops is to increase the use of Roundup herbicide. The claim that Roundup products are safe is a contradiction in terms because a chemical used for its toxic effects on plants cannot be environmentally benign. There is evidence that Roundup can cause harm to the environment and human health even at current levels of use. A new study indicates that glyphosate can be readily released from soil particles, and therefore may leach into water.

- The Northwest Coalition for Alternatives to Pesticides found that products containing glyphosate are acutely toxic to humans. Symptoms include eye and skin irritation, cardiac depression and vomiting (Cox, 'Glyphosate', *Journal of Pesticide Reform*, Fall 1995).
- A report for the Environmental Health Policy Program at the University of California at Berkeley, found that glyphosate was the third most commonly cited cause of pesticide-related illness in agricultural workers.
- The US Fish and Wildlife Service has identified 74 endangered plant species threatened by the use of glyphosate.
- In October 1999, environmental campaigners demanded a Europe-wide ban on Roundup after a EU report was leaked which warned that Roundup could kill insects and spiders vital to agricultural ecosystems (Baldwin, *Guardian*, 13 October 1999).
- Greenpeace and other NGOs have revealed that soya plants sprayed with Roundup contain more plant oestrogens and so are possibly hormone- or endocrine-system disrupters.
- Dairy cows eating RRS are producing milk with different chemical characteristics (higher fat levels) than cows eating regular soya beans.
- A study published in the journal *Cancer* revealed links between glyphosate and non-Hodgkin's lymphoma (a cancer of the lymphatic system).
- Monsanto's ecological risk-assessment for RRS assesses risks only in the US and European context, although RRS is likely to be grown and/or exported to environments of higher ecological risk.
- Irish authorities made public US EPA documents that revealed that Monsanto's Roundup-resistant sugar beets were dying in alarming numbers after having been sprayed with Roundup.

The use of this toxic-to-plants, non-discriminating herbicide threatens to lead to large-scale elimination of indigenous species and cultivated varieties, damaging soil fertility and human health. The claim that soil conservation would be promoted is based on comparing a large monoculture farm using other herbicides, and a similar farm using Roundup. However, the expansion of Roundup Ready crops will be introduced into the biodiversity-rich agro-ecosystems of the Third World. The direct destruction of biodiversity will, in fact, lead to more rapid soil and water erosion, since without cover crops, there will be no protection against the tropical sun and rain. Roundup Ready crops will lead to increased use of Roundup herbicide and hence to the destruction of both cultivated and wild biodiversity. Findings such as these throw into question Monsanto's unsupported assertion of Round up as an environmentally acceptable herbicide.

The genetic engineering option is compared to chemically intensive, large-scale industrial monocultures instead of to ecological organic agriculture, which is the real alternative. Thus, in the case of the Bt. potato, it is stated that genetic engineering leads to a saving of US$6 per acre (per 0.4 hectares) based on insecticide-control costs of $30 to $120 per acre. However, when compared to ecological agriculture, Bt. potato increases the costs by $25 to $115 per acre and correspondingly, also *increases insecticide use*. The industry's assessments give a benefit without calculating the additional costs of seeds and royalties as well as the agrichemical use which is a necessary part of Bt.-resistance management.

Herbicides and pesticides are toxic chemicals aimed at controlling weed and pest problems in crops. However, these reductionist 'solutions' of the Green Revolution have proved non-sustainable. Herbicide residues in soils have led to decline in yields, and pesticide use has led to an increase in pests both through the killing of the pests' predators and the emergence of pesticide-resistance in pests.

Genetic engineering is now deepening the reductionist paradigm of controlling pests through the creation of herbicide-resistant and pest-resistant crops. These applications account for more than 80 per cent of the biotechnology research in agriculture. Their introduction will also lead to increased chemical use if 'superweeds' and 'superpests' are created as a result of biological pollution. This will be further discussed in the next chapter.

The Myth of Safety

Experience has taught us a few simple lessons over the centuries:

- That each time we manipulate nature technologically, there is an ecological impact, whether large or small.
- That the negative impact generated should be internalized in the costs of production. This is the Polluter-Pays Principle.
- That if there is scientific uncertainty about the impact, we should err on the side of caution. This is the Precautionary Principle.

Good science is aware of the ecological impact of new technologies, internalizes the costs of the technologies, and acts cautiously on issues of uncertainty. Bad science is blind to and ignorant about ecology, the Precautionary Principle and the Polluter-Pays Principle. All technologies generate social and environmental costs. However, the costs generated by genetic engineering are different in nature and scale because life forms reproduce and multiply – and disasters unleashed through genetic engineering cannot be halted. Further, since genetic manipulations play with the very fabric of life, the potential of ecological instability is very high.

The potential impact of genetic engineering includes:

- The impact on the organism itself.
- The impact on the ecosystem in which the GMO is released.
- The impact on human society.
- The impact on human health.

Scientifically informed decision-making would be based on knowledge of how to create GMOs and to apply biotechnology to agriculture and medicine, matched with knowledge of the social-ecological impact. However, not only are the ecological risks not being investigated, the knowledge of risks is being suppressed and censored. The right to knowledge and the right to information is a basic right of citizens in democratic society. The right to be free from environmental risk is also a fundamental human right. The human right to environmental safety in the special context of biosafety is, however, being systematically violated by the biotech industry and by governments promoting the interest of industry by sacrificing the obligation to protect the public interest and the environment.

Genetically engineered crops and foods are being launched in a context in which profits are privatized through IPRs. The public is kept deliberately ignorant of the true social costs through the denial of the need for biosafety regulations and the consumers' 'right to know' through the labelling of genetically engineered foods.

Genetically modified foods threaten public health, and have earned themselves the popular label of Frankenstein foods because they contain genes from unrelated organisms – from animals, bacteria and viruses. The anxiety about the impact on health and the ecology of these novel foods is partly founded on the experience of such epidemics as BSE (known as Mad Cow Disease). It is also founded on the basic scientific fact that introducing novel genes into crops will change their physiology and biochemistry, and this could have harmful effects on health.

L-tryptophan is a food supplement, and millions of people in North America have been using it regularly since the 1980s. One producer, Shawo Denko, used genetic engineering to produce L-tryptophan. In late 1989, thousands of North Americans fell ill. Within months dozens had died and thousands were maimed as a result of EMA (eosinophilia-myalgia syndrome). L. R. B. Mann and D. Straton have called the tryptophan disaster 'The Thalidomide of Genetic Engineering' (Third World Network Features, News Release, 19 August 1999).

If a purported single chemical – the natural animic acid tryptophan, better than 98.5 per cent pure and definitely meeting the notorious 'substantial equivalence' test – can turn out when genetically engineered to kill dozens and cripple thousands, what will it take to check properly a potato containing a synthetic 'exact' copy of a gene for a toxin from the African clawed toad? Reference to toads is not a fairy tale in the genetic engineering world. Biotech companies are engineering toxins from the wasps, the cone snail, from the deadly scorpion or the Australian funnel web spider into plants so that plants produce their own poisons. This is supposed to be a solution for pest control, but will render the GM plant toxic, killing not just pests but also beneficial insects. Nothing is known of how safe it is for humans to eat foods containing genes from scorpions, wasps, spiders and snails (Action Aid, *Astra Zeneca and its Genetic Research*, 1999).

Genetically engineered foods have been cleared by agencies on grounds that they are substantially equivalent to their naturally occurring counterparts. Yet, the method of production clearly changes the effect of foods. When yeast was genetically modified to obtain increased fermentation, it was unexpectedly discovered that the metabolite metyl-glyoxal accumulated in toxic and mutagenic concentrations (Inose and Murata, *International Journal of Food Science Technology*, 1995).

Monsanto's transgenic soya was approved for sale in the UK from 1996 by the UK Novel Foods committee as 'substantially equivalent' and therefore safe. However, it was found to have a 26.7 per cent increase in a major allergen, trypsin inhibitor, which is also a growth inhibitor. In an article in the *Journal of Nutrition*, 1996, B. G. Hammand and others reported that when rats were fed the transgenic soya, their growth rate was inhibited.

Dr Arpad Pusztai's research, which created a major controversy in the scientific community, showed that potatoes genetically engineered with snowdrop lectin seemed to suppress the immune responses of young rats and harm the development of vital organs. Dr Pusztai was retired from the Rowett Research Institute in Aberdeen as a result of this work. But Dr S. W. B. Ewen, a senior pathologist at the University of Aberdeen confirmed Dr Pusztai's results through independent experiments, and many scientists rallied to his support. The medical journal the *Lancet* published his study in spite of pressure being brought on the editor. A ban was imposed on growing genetically engineered crops of any kind in the UK for three years. UK laws now require mandatory labelling of all genetically engineered foods.

The consumers' freedom to eat GE-free food is also threatened by the inadvertent contamination of seed, as was the case in Europe in the spring of 2000 when it was found that conventional seed bought from Canadian suppliers included GE varieties.

In genetic engineering, genes are transferred from one organism to the other. This gene transfer can result in the production of new proteins. Food that was safe could therefore become dangerous. Pioneer HiBreed engineered soya with a gene from the brazil nut to improve the protein content. Researchers at the University of Nebraska tested these soya beans on samples of blood serum taken from people allergic to brazil nuts. The tests revealed that if these people had eaten the soya bean, they would have suffered an allergic reaction that could have been fatal. As Marion Nestle stated in the *New England Journal of Medicine*, 1996: 'In the special case of transgenic (GE) soya beans, the donor species was known to be allergenic, serum samples from persons allergic to the donor species were available for testing and the product was withdrawn. The next case could be less ideal and the public less fortunate.'

For a long time, Monsanto claimed that its recombinant bovine growth hormone (rbgh) was safe. Recent research has shown that milk from cows treated with (rbgh) may contribute to enhanced risk of mammary cancer by increasing the concentration of IGF-1 (insulin-like growth factor) in milk (Outwater, et al., *Medical Hypothesis*, 1997; Gebaner, *Anti-cancer Research*, 1998; Hawkinson, et al., *Lancet*, 1998).

Genetically engineered foods can also be hazardous because the vectors used to construct transgenes can infect mammalian cells and resist breakdown in the gut. In a study designed to test the survival of viral DNA in the gut, mice were fed DNA, and large fragments were found to survive the passage through the gut and enter the bloodstream (Schubbert, et al., *Molecular Genetics*). Invasive strains of *Shigella* and *E. coli* can be similarly absorbed. The crossing of species barriers to make transgenic crops and foods also facilitates the crossing of disease barriers across species. As biologist Mae-Wan Ho says:

Natural genetic parasites, like viruses and other transposable elements, proteins and plasmids, are naturally specific to certain species. They have species barriers, genetic barriers. A virus from a pig will not generally attack humans, and so on. What genetic engineering does is to destroy these species barriers. So when you join these viruses and transposable elements from widely different sources, you create similarities to all these different species. You are levelling the gene-transfer barriers that naturally exist. I really am worried about this because since 1993 an increasing number of publications have reported that horizontal gene transfer is responsible for new and bold pathogens arising.

(Quoted in Suzuki, *From Naked Ape to Super Species*)

In a study carried out in Eastern Germany, streptothricin was administered to pigs from 1982. By 1983, plasmid encoding streptothricin-resistance was found in the pig gut-bacteria. By 1984 this had spread to the gut-bacteria of farm workers and their families, and the following year to the general public and pathological streams of bacteria. The antibiotic was withdrawn in 1990, but the prevalence of the resistant plasmid remained high when monitored in 1993. (Tschape, *FEMS Microbiology Ecology*, 1994.)

In 1995, Stephenson and Warnes cautioned, 'The threat of horizontal gene-transfer from recombinant organisms to indigenous ones is very real, and mechanisms exist whereby, at least theoretically, any genetically engineered trait can be transferred to any prokaryotic organism and many eukaryotic ones. (*Biotech*, 1995.)

In 1996, the Advisory Committee on Novel Foods and Processes advised the UK Government to vote against an authorization sought by Novartis for a genetically engineered maize containing an ampicillin-resistant gene. They felt that the presence of this intact marker gene, together with a bacterial promoter gene posed an unacceptable risk (*Ag. Biotech News and Information*). A report in the *New Scientist* of 30 January 1999 confirmed that antibiotic resistance could jump from genetically modified foods to bacteria in the gut.

Dr Mae-Wan Ho in *Genetic Engineering: Dream or Nightmare?* (1997) has identified the following risks to human health from genetically engineered foods:

- Toxic or allergenic effects due to transgene products or interactions of transgene with host genes.
- Vector-mediated spread of antibiotic resistance marker genes to gut bacteria and to pathogens.
- Vector-mediated spread of virulence among pathogens across species by horizontal gene-transfer and recombination.
- Potential for vector-mediated horizontal gene transfer and recombination to create new pathogenic bacteria and viruses.
- Potential of vector-mediated infected cells after ingestion of transgenic foods, to regenerate disease viruses, or for the vector to insert itself into the cell's genome causing harmful or lethal effects including cancer.

Because of the health and environmental risks of so-called Frankenstein Foods, consumers are rejecting genetically engineered foods. The 'new, improved' products, as the biotechnology industry has tried to sell them, are 'new' but not 'improved' in the consumers' view. Through consumer pressure, food retailers and food traders have started to deal in GE-free foods. In April 1999, Unilever, Nestlé and Cadbury announced that they were phasing out genetically modified products globally because of customer resistance. Tesco and the Co-op did the same, joining the other big supermarket chains. In August 1999, Edeka, German's largest retailer declared that it is completely abandoning GE foods. Other large German retailers to go GE-free are Spar and Metro. In September 1999, Brake Bros, Britain's biggest distributor of frozen foods, eradicated GM ingredients from all its products, making it the first wholesale catering supplier to be totally GM free. The group promises that all 2,000 food items it supplies to restaurants, hotels, schools and hospitals will be GM-free.

In Japan, the import of GM soya beans has declined rapidly as food-processing companies shift their purchases to soya beans that have not been genetically modified. The Japanese Government has announced plans to require labelling of products made from

GM crops beginning in April 2001. In August 1999, Kirin, Japan's largest brewer and a leading biotech company, announced that by 2001 it would stop using GM corn to make beer. Sapporo Breweries Ltd, Japan's third largest beer producer also announced that it will stop using GM corn to make beer. Honda Trading Co. is building a plant to bag GE-free soya beans and will contract with US farmers for their production. Fuji Oil Ltd, Japan's largest manufacturer of soya bean protein food products will stop using GM soya bean from April 2000.

When concerns were raised about GM safety, the US government and the biotechnology industry insisted that segregation and labelling of GM foods were not technically possible. Consumer boycotts, however, have made segregation a possibility. In March 1999, two major grain processors, ADM and A. E. Staley Mfg. Co., announced that they would not accept any varieties not approved for import into Europe. ADM started to procure non-GM soya at a premium.

As reported in *Business Week* of 18 October 1999, Dave Borttger a US farmer, like many others in his country, is having to pay for having cultivated GE crops. ADM is offering 8 cents a bushel more for the old-fashioned corn that Borttger grows on half of his land than the gene-spliced corn he grows on the other half. But if testing reveals even a tiny amount of altered gene in the GM-free grain, Borttger will have to pay ADM for the cost of dumping the entire load.

The concerns for safety are leading to a shift in trends. Instead of millions of acres being converted from non-GM to GM crops, the reverse has started to happen.

In the USA the American Corn Growers Association, in an official press release dated 25 August 1999, has proposed that farmers explore the option of planting non-GM crops in the light of the uncertainty caused by GMOs (genetically modified organisms). The consolidated Grain and Barge Company, in a letter to producers, state that consignments containing GMO contamination, 'no matter how trivial, will not be eligible for premium prices as GMO crops become increasingly unsaleable on international markets'. The Canadian Wheat Board has stated that no transgene varieties should be registered for production in Canada. In Brazil, the state of Rio Grande de Sul has declared itself GE-free. In India, hundreds of villages have taken a pledge to be GE-free zones. The people are making their choice clear. They are voting for food freedom and food democracy, food security and food safety.

CHAPTER 3

BIOPOLLUTION AND BIOSAFETY

Biosafety refers to environmental safety in the context of genetic engineering. Genetic engineering risks a new form of pollution or 'contamination', called genetic pollution or biopollution. In certain cases, biopollution can have major health and environmental impacts and create biohazards – dangers threatening biodiversity at the genetic, species or ecosystem level. The introduction of new species into ecosystems is one form of biohazard – invasive species dominate ecosystems and displace native biodiversity. The introduction of exotic genes into organisms is another form of biohazard, since its ecological impacts are unpredictable.

Bioinvasions and Green Plagues

Ecological destabilization is leading to biological invasions of ecosystems by exotic species. Bioinvasions are now recognized as a major ecological problem, and are on the increase with globalization as viruses and seeds are moved across the world on planes and ships.

Zebra mussels, little shellfish the size of a kidney bean, were introduced to North America through the ballast waters of a supertanker around 1986. Zebra mussels clog up pipes and waterways, and multiply at an incredible rate – a single female may release more than five million eggs in the course of a year. It has been estimated that the economic costs of this invasion could be $5 billion by the year 2000. (Lyadyansky, et al., *Bio-Science*, September 1993)

When the Nile perch was introduced into Lake Victoria, 60 per cent of the native fish species disappeared. Indigenous fish accounted for the 76 per cent fish biomass in the lake in 1983, but for only 7 per cent in 1985, while the Nile perch increased from 16 per cent to 90 per cent. Unsurprisingly, the introduction of the exotic Nile perch is considered the main reason for the disappearance of fish diversity in Lake Victoria (Ogutu-Ohwaya, *Invasive Species*, 1999).

In 1956, 54 African queen bees were imported to Brazil from South Africa for breeding programmes. Twenty-six swarms of hybrid bees escaped from the laboratory, and became the 'African killer bees'. Their migration front reached Panama in 1982, Mexico in 1987, Texas in 1990, California in 1993. So far more than 1,000 people have died after being stung by the exotic hybrids. This is twice as many as the victims of the Ebola and Marburg virus infections put together (*Los Angeles Times*, 1 November 1994).

There are many examples of exotic plant species that were introduced into ecosystems where they became invasive. The kundzu plant was introduced into the USA from Japan as a cattlefeed. In the 1930s Civilian Conservation planted thousands of the plants to control soil erosion. The kundzu has overtaken the south-eastern states of the USA and can grow more than 75 feet (23 metres) in a single season.

Parthenium hysterophorus (wild carrot weed) is a noxious weed which has spread to many parts of India, covering in total 5 million hectares (12 million acres). A native of tropical America, it is reported that its seeds came to India with grain shipments from the USA. It was first noticed in Poona in 1951. Since then it has spread like wildfire across the length and breadth of the country. It appeared in Karnataka in 1961, in Kashmir in 1963, in Madhya Pradesh in 1968, in the Western Himalaya in 1970, and in Assam and Rajasthan in 1979. In addition to displacing local biodiversity, the weed causes dermatitis and other allergies. It also affects agricultural crops such as maize, jowar and arhar. A single plant produces more than 10,000 seeds, which travel long distances and can propagate under all kinds of environmental conditions.

The *Lantana camera* was hybridized in Europe in the seventeenth century by using a complex of West Indian and South American species to make attractive flowering plants. Europeans introduced these hybrid *Lantanas* to their colonies in the tropics. Today these plants crowd out native species, invading pastures and forests. The plants are toxic to livestock but produce berries that birds eat and spread. 'Man unwittingly had created and then let loose on the world a green plague.' (Koopowitz and Kaye, *Plant Extinction: A Global Crisis,* 1990.)

The erosion of biodiversity can also facilitate the spread of infectious diseases – in fact, diseases can be viewed as species invasions at the bacterial and viral level. The Kayasanur Forest Syndrome was a fatal disease spread by monkeys into human populations in South India as the forest habitat was destroyed. The theory is often put forward that AIDS had similar beginnings. It is this disease and invasive species model that provides the most relevant lessons for anticipating and assessing the risks of genetic engineering.

Genetic Pollution

In a similar way, genetic engineering could be unleashing new 'green plagues', as genes for herbicide-resistance move into the wild relatives and create 'superweeds', and Bt. crops create 'superpests' by killing predators and contributing to the emergence of pest-resistance.

Genetic engineering has raised concerns for biosafety since the tools for gene-splicing were first developed. There have been two phases in the discussions of risks associated with it. The first was during the time when the techniques of recombinant DNA were emerging. This phase was experimental and work was based on the use of crippled organisms which were not meant to survive in the environment. The main practitioners were university scientists, and, through the Asilomar Declaration in 1972, they themselves called for a moratorium on recombinant DNA research. The second was the 'Wall Street' phase, when scientists who had developed genetic engineering left universities to start biotechnology firms. Concerns for safety were sacrificed to the promise of biotech miracles. This phase is now itself undergoing changes. Genetically engineered organisms are being released for production and consumption on global markets, and the small start-up firms are being bought up by giant chemical corporations. Production is undertaken using ecologically robust organisms. The issues of biosafety are now very different from the days of the Asilomar Declaration.

Laboratory strains of genetically engineered organisms are not designed to survive in an open environment. Therefore we cannot justify extrapolation from laboratory data to ecosystems. Further, existing field tests for safety and risk assessment are not designed to collect environmental data, and test conditions do not proximate production conditions that include commercial scale, varying environments and time scale.

Unlike machines, living organisms have the capacity to organize themselves. Introduced genes can function differently than predicted, and they can move unpredictably into other organisms. Engineering is in fact an inappropriate word for genetic manipulation. Basically, a plant's genome (all of its genes taken together) is a black box. Genetic engineering takes a gene from one black box and forces it into a second black box, hoping that the new gene will take. Most of the time the experiment fails. Once in a thousand times the foreign gene embeds itself in the recipient plant's genome, and the newly modified plant gains the desired trait. But that is all the technicians know. They have no idea where in the receiving plant's genome the new gene has found a home. This fundamental ignorance, combined with the speed and scale at which modified organisms are being released into the global ecosystem, raises a host of questions for the future on the safety of agriculture, of the environment and of human health ('Against the Grain', *Rachel's Weekly*, 18 February 1999).

Transgenes are based on species pollution by definition, since they are formed by crossing species boundaries, mixing genes of species that do not breed and changing the integrity and uniqueness of a species. Ecosystem pollution can occur because genetically engineered crops can change interactions between species, leading to the domination of certain species, and the displacement of others.

Since genes do not exist in isolation but in interaction, the genome is described as fluid, suggesting that the gene has no well-defined continuity or boundaries, the expression of each gene being ultimately dependent on, and entangled with every other gene in the genome. Since the genome is fluid, genes also jump – they can excise and reinsert themselves in different locations in the genomes – jumping genes or transposons were first discovered by geneticist Barbara McClintock more than forty years ago.

Genes can also move from one organism to another, and between species that do not interbreed, a process called 'horizontal gene-transfer'. Horizontal, or lateral, gene-transfer is defined as the nonsexual transfer of genetic information between organisms. Ordinarily gene-transfer takes place vertically from parent to offspring. Horizontal gene-transfer has been identified as the reason for the emergence of antibiotic resistance. The first definitive evidence for this came from DNA sequence analysis of the genes for neomycin-kanamycin resistance to *Staphylococcus aureus*, *Streptococci* and *Campylobacter*. Antibiotic-resistant genes, especially those carried on plasmids and transposons, can, in principle, cross species as well as genera and even kingdoms. Horizontal gene-transfer is also identified as the process behind the emergence of new and old virulent streams of pathogens since the 1980s. A severe infection by *Streptococcus pyogenes* was traced to a toxin encoded by a gene belonging to a bacterial genome.

Genetic engineering can increase the risks of horizontal gene-transfer. Firstly, the vectors used for transferring genes from one organism to another can themselves become mechanisms. These vectors are aggressive hybrids made by joining together bits of natural gene-transfer vectors – viruses, plasmids and transposons. They are designed to be promiscuous, so that they can effectively smuggle genes into cells that would otherwise exclude them. The most common vector used is *Agrobacterium tumefacieus*, which causes cancerous tumours, known as crown galls, in plants. In order to put new genes into plants, such as the 'Roundup Ready' gene in Monsanto soya beans, the gene is first introduced into the DNA of *Agrobacterium* plasmids and the bacteria are then imported into the plants. Monsanto describes this aggressive bacterium as: 'A naturally occurring soil bacterium used to genetically improve plants.' The potential for the *Agrobacterium* plasmid horizontal gene-transfer is unlimited. Yet monitoring such risks is not required under current regulations.

How Biosafety was Sacrificed for Commerce

The international platform for preventing biopollution and ensuring biosafety is the Convention on Biological Diversity signed at the Earth Summit in Rio in 1992. The Biosafety Protocol which was negotiated under Article 19.3 of the Convention is the legally binding instrument that should address issues related to the impact of GMOs on the environment and public health.

The USA has undermined the Biosafety Protocol since 1991 when article 19.3 was being negotiated. It mobilized the Miami Group – consisting of Canada, Australia, Chile, Argentina and Uruguay – to prevent the Protocol from being finalized at Cartagena, Columbia in February 1999. The attempt to prevent an environmental agreement from coming into force was repeated in Vienna in August 1999. However, in February 2000 the negotiations for a Protocol were completed in Montreal. This has, at least for the time being, countered the attempt to move the discussions on biosafety from where they belong – the Biosafety Protocol – to where they do not belong – the WTO, which has neither the mandate nor the capacity for environmental regulation to prevent and prohibit activity causing pollution. Its mandate is to promote trade and remove trade restrictions for products that generate pollution. In the case of GMOs, the pollution generated is biological pollution.

The objective for moving biosafety issues from a multilateral environment agreement, the CBD, to a free-trade agreement, the WTO, was evident in the US proposal of 4 August 1999. It was also reflected in the Ministerial Text of 19 October 1999 for the Seattle WTO conference. The proposal calls for: 'Disciplines to ensure that trade in products of agricultural biotechnology is based on transparent, predictable and timely processes.' Transparency, predictability and timely processes, however, mean different things to different people. It is ironic that the country calling for transparency has actively prevented transparency in the trade of GMOs by refusing the segregation and labelling of GM products. Decisions on trade in GMOs have been opaque from the perspective of citizens and consumers. For citizens, transparency implies transparency of corporation action.

For corporations, transparency implies their easy access to government decisions. The USA is clearly referring to the latter, while the anti-GM movements refer to the former.

The USA has repeatedly used WTO rules and disputes as a threat to European countries who refuse GM/biotech foods. On 18 June 1997, the biotech and agriculture industry wrote to President Clinton suggesting that it was critical that the EU understand at the highest level that the USA would consider any such trade barrier unacceptable and subject to challenge in WTO. In June 1997, the US Trade Representative warned the EU Agriculture Commissioner not to continue with proposals to require the labelling of genetically modified organisms (GMOs) or their segregation from regular products. The Trade Representative told the Senate Agriculture Committee that the USA cannot tolerate a step which would cause a major disruption in US exports to the EU. In a letter to the US Secretary on 12 June 1997, American agribusiness corporations stated that the segregation of crops for labelling is both scientifically unjustified and commercially unfeasible. However, after a number of leading food processors, such as Nestlé, Unilever, Gerber, Heinz, and Kirin announced they would not use GM ingredients in their foods, and major European supermarkets announced their intention to ban GM foods, leading grain companies such as Archer Daniels Midland and Consolidated Grain and Barge told farmers and grain merchants to segregate crops from new GM crops.

According to US industry, labelling of foods violates the GATT agreement on free trade. The Sanitary and Phyto-Sanitary Measures in GATT are thus viewed by industry as protecting their interests. The consumers' democratic rights to information cannot be decided by arbitrary technocratic and corporate decision-making on what is 'sound science' and what is not.

Sound Science or Unsound Science?

'Sound science' has become a mantra for protecting the biotechnology industry by banishing safety regulations from the commercialization of genetic engineering. This was the phrase used by the industry in the letter to President Clinton at the G7 Summit in Denver 18 June 1997. It is the language of a *Wall Street Journal* editorial of 6 November 1997 that accuses Europe of practising 'junk science' in banning the import of hormone-fed beef, and referring to the WTO decision. The US Agricultural Secretary, Dan Glickman, stated categorically that the United States will stand behind its genetically engineered foods and will oppose any European labelling requirements as a trade violation. According to Glickman: 'We've got to make sure that sound science prevails, not what I call historic culture, which is not based on sound science. Europe has a much greater sensitivity to the culture of food as opposed to the science of food. But in the modern world, we just have to keep the pressure on the science. Good science must prevail in these decisions.'

The safety debate has been suppressed again and again by bad science parading as 'sound science'. One of the unscientific strategies used to extinguish the safety discussion is to define a novel organism or novel food created through genetic engineering as 'substantially equivalent' to conventional organisms and foods. However, a GMO is different because it has genes from unrelated organisms – it cannot, therefore, be treated as equivalent to a non-genetically engineered organism. In fact, the biotechnology industry itself gives up the claim of 'substantial equivalence' when it claims patents on GMOs on grounds of novelty.

Officials of the Food and Drug Administration had repeatedly cautioned that foods produced through biotechnology entail different risks from their conventionally produced counterparts. In spite of scientific warnings, President Bush and the US government issued a 'no labelling' and 'no safety testing' policy on gene-altered foods in 1992. The false assumption of 'substantial equivalence' was introduced by President Bush in US policy immediately after Rio to blunt the call for biosafety regulation. It was later formalized and introduced in 1993 by OECD (UN Organization for Economic Co-operation and Development), and subsequently endorsed by FAO (UN Food and Agriculture Organization) and WHO (World Health Organization). The OECD document states:

For foods and food components from organisms developed by the application of modern biotechnology, the most practical approach to the determination is to consider whether they are substantially equivalent to analogous food products if such exist. The concept of substantial equivalence embodies the idea that existing organisms used as foods, or as a source of food, can be used as the basis for comparison when assessing the safety of human consumption of a food or food component that has been modified or is new.

(Safety Evaluation of Food derived by Modern Biotechnology, Paris 1993)

Apart from being vague, this definition is unsound. Foods with Bt. toxin genes are not the same as foods without. Herbicide-resistant crops are different from existing varieties because they have new genes for resistance to herbicide. An article by Marc Lappé and others in the *Journal of Medicinal Food* (1999) has established that Monsanto Roundup Ready soya beans change the levels of phytoestrogens by 12 to 14 per cent. To treat these differences as insignificant when it is a question of safety, and as significant when it is a question of patentability, is totally unscientific. As Millstone, Brunner and Mayer have stated in 'Beyond Substantial Equivalence' (*Nature*, 7 October 1999):

Substantial equivalence is a pseudo-scientific concept because it is a commercial and political judgement masquerading as if it were scientific. It is, moreover, inherently anti-scientific because it was created primarily to provide an excuse for not requiring biochemical or toxicological tests. It, therefore, serves to discourage and inhibit potentially informative scientific research.

Politics and profits parading as science has been institutionalized into the WTO trade systems. Through the Sanitary or Phyto-Sanitary (SPS) agreement, and the Technical Barriers to Trade (TBT), WTO has made one body, the Codex Alimentarius Commission, the ultimate decision-making body in disputes related to food safety. The participants are mainly Northern countries and industries, with the South and citizens heavily under-represented. The biotech industry and rich countries therefore determine Codex decisions. The WTO rules state that disputes will be arbitrated on grounds of 'sound science'. However, as the assumption of substantial equivalence shows, what is 'sound science' can be very unscientific and unsound.

The biotech industry can use WTO to prevent people from exercising their basic right to safe food. Article 2.2 of the SPS Agreement states that all sanitary and phyto-sanitary measures will be based on scientific principles and will not be maintained without sufficient scientific evidence. This goes totally against the Precautionary Principle embodied in Principle 15 of the 1992 Rio Declaration on Environment and Development: 'When there are threats of serious or irreversible damage, lack of full scientific certainty shall not be used as a reason for postponing cost-effective measures to prevent environmental degradation.'

Biotechnology exemplifies the clash between profits and safety, between commerce and conservation, between greed and need between trade treaties like GATT/WTO and environmental treaties such as CBD. The outcome of this conflict will determine the future of our health and environment. It will also determine whether global corporations will rule our lives, protected by WTO and governments, or will be governed by rules of justice and sustainability, and accountable.

Biopollution

As the Green Revolution miracle fades into ecological disaster, the biotechnology revolution is being heralded as an ecological miracle for agriculture. But, genetic engineering is unleashing biological and genetic pollution, while in addition spreading agrichemicals in agro-ecosystems where they have not been used before. Chemically intensive farming in the last forty years has led to severe environmental threats to plant, animal and human life. In the popular mind 'chemical' has come to be associated with 'ecologically hazardous'. The ecologically safe alternatives have been commonly labelled as 'biological'. Biotechnology has benefited from falling into the 'biological' category. Biotech industry has described its agricultural innovations as 'Ecology Plus'.

It is, however, more fruitful to contrast the ecological with the engineering paradigm, and to locate biotechnology in the latter. The engineering paradigm offers technological fixes for complex problems, and, by ignoring the complexity, generates new ecological problems that are later defined away as 'unanticipated side-effects' and 'negative externalities'. Within the engineering ethos it is impossible to anticipate the ecological breakdown that an engineering intervention can cause. Biotechnology cannot provide the framework for an assessment of its ecological impact on agriculture.

Unlike toxic hazards, biohazards multiply and have no recall. As Elaine Ingham, Professor of Soil Ecology at Oregon State University, has stated:

> Any engineered organism to be released into the real world, free from the controlled laboratory situation, must be treated as the potential hazard that it is. The biotechnology industry needs to step back and make certain that the biological potential of the organisms being altered, both before and after alterations, is recognized and understood. After all, organisms are capable of reproduction, of increasing in number and spreading. Human-produced chemicals may have posed problems to the environment but at least chemicals, whether organic or inorganic, did not reproduce. One molecule of a problem chemical remained one molecule and did not replicate and become a million problems.

One example of the risks of genetic pollution was the case of a genetically engineered soil organism, *Klepsiella planticola*, which had been designed to digest biomass and produce ethanol as a way of getting rid of farm wastes and producing alternative sources of energy. The German biotech company applied to the USA for field tests, and Oregon State University took up the trials. Elaine Ingham and Michael Holmes compared the results of applying the genetically engineered *Klepsiella* and the naturally occurring *Klepsiella* to soils and crops. Every plant grown with the GE *Klepsiella* died. If released, it could have killed all plant life and destroyed agriculture and food production. What prevented this was the independent research by independent scientists who assessed the impact in living soil and not sterile soils, as is usually the case. As Elaine Ingham admits, 'If we hadn't done this research, the *Klepsiella* would have passed the approval process for commercial release.'(Holmes, et al., *Applied Soil Ecology*, vol. 326, 1998.)

The Oregon experiment was among the very few ecological assessments of the impact of GMOs on the environment. Promoters of genetic engineering often cite that thousands of GM trials have taken place and they have established safety. However, safety assessments have not been carried for any of the crops that cover millions of acres. The false assumption of 'substantial equivalence' of GMOs and non-engineered organisms establishes a strategy of deliberate ignorance. Ignorance of risks is then treated as proof of safety. 'Don't look – don't see' leads to total lack of information about the ecological impacts of genetic engineering.

It is often claimed that there have been no adverse consequences from over 500 field releases in the US. However, the term 'releases' is completely misleading. Those tests were largely not scientific tests of realistic ecological concerns, yet 'this sort of nondata on nonreleases has been cited in policy circles as though 500 true releases have now informed scientists that there are no legitimate scientific concerns'. (Rissler and Mellon, *The Ecological Risks of Engineered Crops*, 1996).

Recently, for the first time, the data from the US Department of Agriculture field trials were evaluated to see whether they support the safety claims. The Union of Concerned Scientists (UCS) who conducted the evaluation found that the data collected by the USDA on small-scale tests had little value for commercial risk-assessment. Many reports fail to even mention – much less measure – environmental risks. Of those reports that allude to environmental risk, most have only visually scanned field plots looking for stray plants or isolated test crops from relatives. The UCS concluded that the observations that 'nothing happened' in those hundreds of tests do not say much. In many cases, adverse impacts are subtle and would never be registered by scanning a field. In other cases, failure to observe evidence of the risk is due to the contained conditions of the tests. Many test crops are routinely isolated from wild relatives, a situation that guarantees no outcrossing. The UCS cautioned that 'care should be taken in citing the field test record as strong evidence for the safety of genetically engineered crops'.

It is also frequently argued that millions of acres planted under genetically modified crops is evidence of testing and safety and proof of consumer acceptance. However, in the absence of labelling, American consumers were unaware that they were consuming GM foods. And GM crops spread because of absence of testing. For example, Bt. toxin is treated as a pesticide by EPA (US Environment Protection Agency), but it is not treated as a food additive or pesticide by FDA (US Food and Drug Administration). Neither EPA nor FDA test Bt. crops for safety (Michael Pollan, *New York Times*, 25 October 1998).

Genetically engineered transgenic crops can contribute to genetic pollution or biological pollution in many ways:

- In herbicide-resistant varieties, transgenes can spread to wild and weedy relatives, creating superweeds.
- Contamination or pollution of biodiversity can destroy the unique characteristics of diverse species.
- Transgenic crops engineered to produce pesticides can lead to evolution of resistance in major insect pests, creating superpests.
- Toxins from the genetically engineered crop can kill beneficial species.

GMOs can also spread disease. Breeding plants resistant to viral infections by inserting virus genes in the plant genome can create new superviruses which have new hosts and new properties (Greene and Allison, 'Viruses and Transgenic Crops', *Science*, 1994).

Genetic pollution or biopollution can also occur through horizontal gene-transfer. Horizontal gene-transfer is the nonsexual transfer of genetic information between organisms. One such case is the sudden 'jumping' of a genetic parasite belonging to yeast, a favourite subject for genetic engineers, into many unrelated species of higher plants.

Our knowledge at the genetic level is too immature to assess the probability or consequences of such horizontal gene-transfer, and the genetic pollution resulting from it. Little has been done to understand the ecology of genes, though much effort has gone into the engineering of genes without any knowledge of the impact of genetically engineered organisms on other organisms and the environment. The lack of knowledge has been taken as proof of safety when it is, in fact, ignorance of biohazards.

Creating Superweeds and Superpests

Two applications of genetic engineering in agriculture account for most plantings and trials – the first is to make crops resistant to herbicides, and the second is to build pesticide-producing properties into plants. Both 'herbicide-resistant' and 'pest-resistant' strategies pose major threats to biodiversity and the environment.

TABLE 2
Global Area of Transgenic Crops (million hectares)

Trait	1997	%	1998	%
Herbicide-resistant	6.9	63	19.8	71
Insect-resistant	4.0	36	7.7	28
Others	<0.1	<1	<0.1	1
Global Total	11.0	100	28.8	100

Source: Clive James, *Global Review of Commercialized Transgenic Crops*, International Society for Acquisition of Agbiotech Applications (ISAAA), 1998

Herbicide-resistant crops can create superweeds by the transfer of resistant traits to wild and weedy relatives through hybridization and cross-pollination. Research in Denmark has shown that oilseed rape can hybridize up to 93 per cent with wild relatives (*American Journal of Botany*, 1994). Wild beets have become a major problem in European sugar beet production since the 1970s. Genetically engineering sugar beet to be herbicide-resistant can only be a temporary solution to the weed beet problem since gene exchange can occur between transgenic sugar beets and weed beets. This would broaden the niche for weeds and create superweeds resistant to herbicides. The efficacy of herbicide-resistant crops would therefore be totally undermined (Bondry, et al., *Theoretical Applied Genetics*, 1993).

Scientists at the National Institute of Agricultural Botany in the UK discovered the first GM superweeds, following the spread of pollen from a GM trial crop to wild turnip plants. As Marie Woolf of the London *Independent* reports (18 April 1999), 'Some of the "Frankenstein" plants, which had inherited their GM parents' herbicide-resistant genes, were able to breed.'

When introduced to regions such as China, Taiwan, Japan, Korea and the former USSR, where wild relatives of soya are found, Monsanto's Roundup Ready soya bean could transfer the herbicide-resistant genes to wild relatives leading to new weed problems. The hazards of gene-transfer to wild relatives are higher in the Third World, because these regions are home to much of the world's biodiversity. As the US Academy of Sciences' 1989 guide 'Field Testing Genetically Modified Organisms' states:

Temperate North America, especially the United States, includes the home ranges for very few crops, as US agriculture is based largely on crops of foreign origin. This paucity of crops derived from North American sources means there will be relatively few opportunities for hybridization between crops and wild relatives in the United States. The incidence of hybridization between genetically modified crops and wild relatives can be expected to be lower here than in Asia Minor, South-east Asia, the Indian subcontinent, and South America, and greater care may be needed in the introduction of genetically modified crops in those regions.The native biodiversity richness of the Third World thus increases the environmental risks of genetic pollution from introduced genetically modified species.

University of Chicago scientists have shown that transgenic crops have a higher tendency to outcross and transfer genes to related crops. Genetically engineered (GE) plants were 20 times more likely to cross with related species compared to conventionally bred plants, in spite of both having the same gene for herbicide-resistance (*Gene Exchange*, Fall/Winter 1998). Research in Germany has shown that genes from GE crops can be transferred to crops in fields 200 metres away, about 660 feet (*Gene Watch Briefing*, May 1998).

Research is also showing that pollen from GE crops remains fertile over longer distances than expected. A study found that even at sites 400 metres (1300 feet) from the GE plots, as many as 7 per cent of the seeds were herbicide-resistant. At 100 metres (330 feet), between 8 and 28 per cent were resistant (*New Scientist*, 17 April 1999).

Plants with the introduced transgene are not fragile. They are robust and produce as many seeds as unmodified counterparts (*Gene Exchange*, Fall/Winter 1998). The threats of genetic and biological pollution are therefore real and serious. While genetic engineering has nothing to show in terms of its proclaimed objectives of increasing yields and decreasing chemical use, the risks that were denied are becoming more and more evident through independent scientific research. This is why there is a global call for a five-year freeze on genetically engineered organisms.

Just as herbicide-resistance can create superweeds, pest-resistance in GE plants can create superpests. Toxin-producing genes from the naturally occurring organism *Bacillus thuringiensis* are being added to a wide range of crops to enable the plants to produce their own insecticide. Monsanto sells its Bt. potato as 'Nature Mark' in Canada. Hendrik Verfaillie, Monsanto's president, speaking at the National Academy of Sciences in Washington, D.C., on 30 October 1997, describes it as a plant using 'sunshine, air and soil nutrients to make a biodegradable, protein that affects just one specific insect pest, and only those individual insects that actually take a bite of the plants'.

- The Bt. plant does not merely use 'sunshine, air and soil nutrients', it has a gene from *Bacillus thuringiensis* which produces the Bt. toxin.
- The so called 'biodegradable protein' is actually a toxin which the gene continuously produces in the plant.
- Insect pests like the cotton bollworm that destroy cotton can actually

evolve resistance because of continuous release of the toxin and hence become 'superpests'.

- The Bt. crop does not affect 'just one specific insect pest'. Beneficial insects like bees and ladybirds can be seriously affected.

The primary justification for the genetic engineering of Bt. into crops is that this will reduce the use of insecticides. A Monsanto brochure with a picture of a few worms stated, 'You will see these in your cotton and that's OK. Don't spray.' However, in Texas Monsanto faces a lawsuit filed by twenty-five farmers over Bt. cotton planted on 18,000 acres which suffered cotton bollworm damage and on which farmers had to use pesticides. In 1996, 2 million acres in the USA were planted with Monsanto's Bt. transgenic cotton called Bollgard, but cotton bollworms were found to have infested thousands of acres of it in Texas.

The question is not whether superpests will be created by the Bt. crops, but when they will become dominant. The fact that the US Environment Protection Agency (EPA) requires *refugia* of non-engineered crops to be planted near the GE crops reflects the real dangers of creating resistant strains of insects. The widespread use of crops containing Bt. could accelerate the development of insect resistance to Bt. used for organic pest control. Already eight species of insects have developed resistance to Bt. toxins, either in the field or laboratory, including diamond back moth, Indian meal moth, tobacco budworm, colorado potato beetle and two species of mosquitoes. The GE Bt. crops express the toxin throughout the growing season. Long-term exposure to Bt. toxin could lead to selection for resistance in all stages of the insect pest on all parts of the plant for the entire season. Owing to this risk, EPA offers only conditional and temporary registration of varieties producing Bt., and requires up to 40 per cent *refugia* with Bt. cotton, i.e. 40 per cent of the cotton planted is to be conventional and does not express the Bt. toxin. It therefore acts as a refuge for insects to survive and breed, and keeps the overall level of resistance in the population low. Even with *refugia*, insect resistance will evolve in as little as three to four years.

While the Monsanto literature states that farmers will not have to use pesticides, the reality is that the management of resistance requires continued use of non-Bt. cotton and pesticide sprays. This leads to rapid development of superpests and the destruction of their natural predators. In Andhra Pradesh in India the 1998 cotton crop failed, Five hundred farmers committed suicide, and Bandi Kalavathi of Venkatapur village was one of them. She was in debt for over $1,000 from buying pesticides for her four acres (1.6 hectares). The cotton catastrophe in Andhra Pradesh will no doubt be used to promote Bt. cotton as a miracle cure for pest problems. But in laboratory tests it has been found that the two pest species that destroyed the Andhra Pradesh cotton crop can evolve resistance to Bt. toxins engineered into Bt. cotton. This shows how vulnerable our agriculture has become – ecological problems need ecological solutions, not magic-bullet technologies.

A study at Cornell University, published in *Nature* 20 May 1999, has shown that Bt. corn killed the larvae of Monarch butterflies, dubbed by the media the 'Bambi of the insect world'. A recent study in Switzerland found that lacewings, which prey on corn pests, suffered maldevelopment and increased mortality when fed corn-borers raised on Bt. maize (Hilbech, et al., in *Environmental Ecology*, 4 August 1998). Bees and other pollinators are also affected. When given sugar solutions with protease inhibitors, which are used to create resistance to insects in transgenic oilseed rape, bees were found to have difficulties learning to distinguish the different smells of flowers (Tudge, *The Engineer in the Garden*, 1993). The Scottish Crop Research Institute at Dundee found that ladybirds fed on aphids that had been feeding on transgenic potatoes laid fewer eggs and lived half as long as those on a normal diet (Brich, et al., *Annual Report*, 1996–97). At New York University researchers found that Bt. toxin from transgenic crops does not disappear when added to soils. Unlike natural Bt., it is not degraded by microbes, nor does it lose the capacity to kill insects. Soil organisms in the soil that degrade organic matter could be harmed by this toxin. The accumulation of transgenic Bt. in the soil poses a major threat to soil ecology (*Gene Exchange*, Fall/ Winter 1998).

The pollution from transgenic crops is spreading through cross-pollination and hybridization, as well as through vertical gene-flow through the food chain. There are no biosafety regulations to stop this genetic pollution. In India, the buffer zone in GE trials is a mere 5 metres (about 16½ feet). In the UK it is 200 metres (about 660 feet). But the canola seed from Canada introduced into Europe had been contaminated in spite of a 800-metre (2,600-feet) buffer zone. The UK Minister for the Environment, Michael Meacher had to admit that bees, which may fly up to 9 kilometres (6 miles) in search of nectar, cannot be expected to observe a 'no-fly zone' (Greenpeace and the Soil Association, *The True Cost of Food,* 1999). A study by the National Pollen Research Unit in 1999 shows that wind can carry viable maize pollen hundreds of kilometres in 24 hours. Transgenic pollen was found 4.5 km (nearly 3 miles) from a field of GM oilseed rape in the Oxfordshire. This was at least 20 times over the limit set by the regulatory agencies (Reuters, 30 September 1999).

Biological pollution implies that the possibility of producing uncontaminated organic food is destroyed. In 1999, 87,000 packs of organic Tortilla chips worth over £100,000 were recalled and destroyed because they were found to be contaminated with DNA from transgenic maize. In a radio programme on 31 January 1999, Nick Brown, UK Minister of Agriculture, asserted that, 'The government is absolutely committed to making sure that those who do not want to eat crops that have been cross-contaminated, are to have their rights in this protected as well.' However, as long as ecological research is hampered by lack of funding for science in the public interest, and as long as laws to prevent genetic pollution are not put in place, people's right to be free of biopollution will be denied.

The building-up of pest-resistance undermines the use of natural Bt. in organic agriculture. This is the reason that legal action against the EPA was filed in Washington in September 1999 by Greenpeace International, the International Federation of Organic Agriculture Movements (world organization of organic farmers, certifiers, producers, retailers, with 650 members in over 100 countries), the Sierra Club, the National Family Farm Coalition, California Certified Organic

Farmers, the Rural Advancement Foundation International (RAFI), the Institute for Agriculture and Trade Policy and over twenty organic farmers' organizations. The central demands of the petition are that the EPA cancels registration of all genetically engineered plants that contain the Bt. pesticide, and stops taking new registrations. Further, that it issues an impact statement analysing the registering of GE plants that express Bt.

In India, the Research Foundation for Science, Technology and Ecology (RFSTE) has legally challenged the Bt. cotton trials of Monsanto-MAHYCO (Maharastra Hybrid Company, set up by Monsanto as a joint venture). These trials were illegal since they bypassed the rules of the Environment Protection Act. Since India is home to cotton biodiversity, GE cotton poses higher risks of genetic pollution to agriculture and biodiversity.

Biopolluters Should Pay

Some of the risks of biopollution and genetic pollution created by the release of genetically modified organisms are now well known and well established empirically. Movements against genetic engineering have grown and spread across the world. They are based on the unpredictability of the impact of GMOs on the environment and public health, and they have made the trade in GMOs unpredictable. Consumer rejection has forced retailers and processors to become GE-free, which in turn has forced traders to segregate and offer premiums for GE-free crops. The unpredictability of trade in GMOs is a fallout of the environmentally irresponsible manner in which GM crop-planting was spread to cover millions of acres, and GM foods were introduced into global markets without any biosafety regulation.

The challenge at Seattle in November 1999 was to stop the further deregulation of GM trade, already characterized by political and environmental unaccountability, and to stop the trend of transforming environmental problems needing environmental solutions into trade problems with further trade deregulation presented as the solution. An important principle of environmental protection is the Polluter-Pays Principle. Genetic engineering creates the potential for biopollution. This requires that we put in place regulatory systems that prevent biopollution, and make the polluter pay when it does occur. However, while the commercial application of genetic engineering is growing exponentially, the knowledge of its ecological impact is still in its infancy. This has come about for many reasons. Firstly, most biologists are now financed through corporate grants as public financing of research dwindles. An independent publicly financed research community is therefore fast disappearing. Biosafety requires a large body of independent research. This expertise is different from the expertise of constructing transgenic organisms. Refrigerator manufacturers are not experts in ozone depletion, automobile makers are not experts in climate change and genetic engineers are not experts in biopollution.

While biosafety cannot be left in the hands of the biotech industry, the industry should bear the costs of independent research by putting a major share of its investments in a publicly held 'Biosafety Fund'. Meantime, since we do not have complete knowledge of impacts, we should err on the side of caution and act according to the Precautionary Principle. This is why scientists and citizens across the world are calling for a five-year freeze on commercialization of GMOs. This will give time for our research and regulatory systems to catch up with the challenge of biosafety and become scientifically and politically equipped to prevent biopollution.

Since biopollution occurs when GMOs are not 'contained' in a closed environment, it is the field trials and planting of GM crops that environmentalists seek to 'freeze', not the production of medicines under contained conditions. The 'freeze' is to accelerate and expand research so that molecular biology is contextualized as gene ecology and our knowledge grows beyond reductionist prisons. The tools offered by the new sciences, such as DNA fingerprinting and genetic identification, are also useful for deepening our understanding of the ecology of genes. Commerce should be guided by knowledge, not the other way around.

CHAPTER 4

HAVING OUR CAKE AND EATING IT TOO

Feeding the world and conserving biodiversity are often seen as opposing and conflicting objectives. Food security is the most frequently cited justification for the destruction of biodiversity through industrialized agriculture. In 1995 the UN Plant Genetics Resources Conference in Leipzig identified the replacement of many traditional crop varieties with 'modern varieties' as the single most important reason for the disappearance of diversity in agriculture. But the conservation of diversity is necessary if we are to end hunger and poverty, and the solutions offered by the biodiversity approach are not just short-term fixes with unacceptably high long-term ecological costs. Biodiversity allows us to maximize food production while helping us maintain ecosystems and renew ecological cycles. It allows us to have our cake and eat it too.

A one-dimensional paradigm based on a 'monoculture of the mind' reduces biodiversity to single functions of single species, and leads to the promotion of utilization patterns that consume and destroy biodiversity and replace it with monocultures. But biodiversity embodies multiple species in multiple interactions performing multiple functions, and if productivity is measured multidimensionally, diversity-based systems are highly productive.

A diverse and species-rich rainforest sustains ecosystems and ecological cycles. It provides food, shelter and healing for many different species. However, it is considered 'unproductive' in the dominant concept of modern forestry, which advocates monocultures, such as eucalyptus for the paper and pulp industry.

A biodiversity-based farm is highly productive when measured in terms of diversity of functions and diversity of outputs. But agriculture is converted into large-scale monocultures, maintained through the intensive use of chemicals and energy, whose ecological impact further destroys biodiversity.

The bhimal (*Grewia optiva*), a popular farm tree in the Himalayas, is a multi-purpose tree whose leaves provide fodder for farm animals in the dry season, and whose branches provide fibre for ropes, fuel for cooking and the ingredients for shampoo. Its roots conserve soil and water, and stabilize the terraced fields. But industrial agricultural experts would say that it should be removed to increase crop yields.

Mustard has always been intercropped with wheat in India. Its leaves are a rich and free source of vitamin A, and cooked as *sarson ka saag* with *Makki ki roti* (corn bread) it is a winter favourite throughout north India. The seeds are a rich source of oil used for cooking, for massage and for lighting. The oilcake is a nutritious cattle food. The Green Revolution, however, defines wheat intercropped with mustard as lowering productivity, and thus destroys the multidimensional and sustainable productivity of mixed cropping.

In the coastal regions of Kerala, rice and shrimp are cropped in a rotational system called *Chemmeenkettu* which has been sustained over centuries. The biomass from the rice feeds the shrimp, the shrimp-droppings fertilize the rice. Agencies such as the World Bank see this as lowering shrimp productivity and have therefore financed the introduction of industrial shrimp farming, which requires intensive feeding, causes heavy pollution and destroys the fragile coastal ecosystems within a year or two. Shrimp yields do increase in that short period, but at the cost of rice, mangroves and fisheries, and also of sustainability. The destruction of mangroves has been identified as a major cause of the highly damaging impact of the Orissa cyclone in 1999 which killed many thousands (Shiva and Karir, *Chemmeenkettu*, 1996; Shiva and Emani, *Climate Change and the Orissa Cyclone*, 1999).

In the one-dimensional way of thinking, the monoculture of the mind, if human needs are to be met then nature must be destroyed. If food is to be produced, biodiversity must be destroyed. On the other hand, in a multifunctional diversity-based world view, it is possible to use biodiversity sustainably while conserving it. It is possible to meet human needs without depriving other species. The false conflict between diversity and productivity disappears as soon as our thinking becomes multidimensional – as soon as it is based on diversity as a way of seeing and relating to the world.

As Thomas Kuhn has shown in *The Structure of Scientific Revolutions* (1962), 'quantity' is not paradigm-independent. 'More' or 'less' are theory-laden, paradigm-dependent terms, and have opposite meanings in the monoculture paradigm and the biodiversity paradigm. A Kuhnian scientific revolution is currently under way in agriculture following the paradigm shift arising from looking at the world through the laws of biodiversity. The dominant monoculture paradigm is being replaced by biodiversity-based alternatives Three indicators of the scientific revolution identified by Kuhn are apparent. Firstly, there is incommensurability of concepts and categories. Secondly, there is an accumulation of anomalies in the dominant paradigm whereby the current paradigm is unintentionally generating evidence against itself. Thirdly, the old guard is resisting change in spite of the accumulation of evidence calling for a paradigm shift.

Research on diverse agricultural systems is showing that there are no neutral facts independent of the theoretical context in which they are measured. 'Yield', 'productivity,' 'growth' are all theory-dependent. When a paradigm shift occurs, the meaning and measure of 'yield', 'productivity' and 'growth' change. The one-dimensional reductionist thinking that destroys diversity sees trees as mere pulpwood, crops as commodities and cows as milk or meat machines. In the diversity paradigm, trees conserve soil and water, they create microclimate, they are the home of diverse species. Crops produce food and nourishment for humans and other animals. And cows are the source of renewable soil fertility and energy. When these diverse functions and relationships are taken into account, native species and indigenous crops and cattle are not 'unproductive'.

Contrary to the dominant way of thinking, productivity and diversity are not inversely but directly correlated. Biodiversity contributes to sustainable production both by allowing us to shift from external inputs, such as chemical fertilizers and pesticides which destroy the environment, and by increasing output of nutrition per acre. The combination of higher outputs and lower costs also improves the farmers' economy. This biodiversity contributes to sustainability, food security and livelihood security.

Sustainability and Saving the Planet

Non-sustainability of industrial agriculture is based on the heavy use of synthetic fertilizers and pesticides, which function like ecological narcotics in the sense that the more they are used the more they have to be used because they destroy nature's processes for the renewal of soil fertility and the control of pests. Chemical fertilizers destroy soil fertility by destroying soil structure and depleting the soil of essential micronutrients. Pesticides destroy friendly species, which control pests, and contribute to the emergence of resistance in pests.

Straw, considered a waste product in industrial agriculture, has an important role to play in the sustainable renewal of the soil's fertility and in the provision of food for livestock. If the output of straw is taken into account, indigenous crop varieties are not low-yielding but high-yielding. When new dwarf varieties are designed to subordinate straw production, the multiple-resource functions of crops are destroyed. Changes in the structure of straw in the 'high-yielding' varieties make it useless for thatch – the hard stalks of the dwarf varieties do not prevent rain from leaking through the roof. This leads to increased use of cement and mining of limestone. Moreover, the hard stalks are useless as fodder. According to A.K. Yegna Iyengar, a leading authority on agriculture:

> As an important fodder for cattle and in fact as the sole fodder in many tracts, the quantity of straw obtainable per acre is important in this country. Some varieties which are good yielders of grains suffer from the drawback of being low in respect to straw.
>
> (*Field Crops of India*, 1944)

Problems with fodder production are not limited to the Third World. A dairy farmer in the UK connected the displacement of traditional barley varieties with a scarcity of fodder, leading to industrial feed made up, in part, of the ground-up parts of other animals – an unnatural and dangerous food source that is blamed for the epidemic of BSE, known as Mad Cow Disease.

According to M. S. Swaminathan in *Science and the Conquest of Hunger* (1983):

> High-yielding varieties of wheat and rice are high-yielding because
> they can use efficiently larger quantities of nutrients and water than
> the earlier strains, which tended to lodge or fall down if grown in soils
> with good fertility.... They thus have a 'harvest index' (i.e. the ratio of
> the economic yield to the total biological yield) which is more favourable
> to man. In other words, if a high-yielding strain and an earlier tall
> variety of wheat both produce, under a given set of conditions,
> 1,000 kg of dry matter, the high-yielding strain may partition this dry
> matter into 500 kg for grain and 500 kg for straw. The tall variety,
> on the other hand, may divert 300 kg for grain and 700 kg for straw.

This elimination of organic matter reduces the capacity of agricultural land to conserve soil and water. Drought and desertification results.

The Green Revolution, financed by the World Bank, has contributed to drought vulnerability by displacing drought-resistant local varieties and replacing them with thirsty seeds which have a high response to chemicals but need three to four times more water than indigenous seeds. In India native wheat requires 12 inches (about 300 mm) of water while Green Revolution varieties need 36 inches (about 900 mm). Jowar and bajra, the traditional crops of Rajasthan and Gujrat need only 20 inches (500 mm) but rice requires 47 inches (1,200 mm). In terms of water-use, millets, which have been referred as 'inferior grains', are twice to three times more efficient than rice. Indigenous crops produce far more nutrition per unit of water than Green Revolution monocultures. Bajra has twice as much protein and iron, three times more minerals, four times as much calcium than rice. But bajra requires only 500 mm of water compared to 1,200 mm for rice. Water-use efficiency in terms of nutrition output is therefore six to ten times higher for bajra than rice. Millets are more productive than rice both in terms of food security and water security. Yet rice acreages have spread, while millet cultivation has dramatically declined, increasing water demand and water withdrawal. Non-sustainable agricultural technologies play a large part in the creation of drought and water scarcity.

The shift from organic manure to chemical fertilizers has also made our soils vulnerable to drought and desertification. Organic manure reduces runoff by 50 per cent. Soil loss can be reduced by 6 tonnes per hectare with 6 tonnes per hectare of organic matter. Organic residues provide food for earthworms and microorganisms which increase the water-holding capacity of soils.

The long-term solution to drought lies in water conservation both through water-harvesting and through the promotion of sustainable ecological agriculture based on biodiversity. This prevents runoff, increases the moisture-holding capacity of soils, reduces the risk of crop failure and reverses the life-threatening processes of drought and desertification which have already engulfed large areas of the planet.

The risk of crop failure is increased by the monocultures typical of Green Revolution practices. Sole-cropped sorghum has been found to fail once in eight years, and pigeon pea once in five years, but a sorghum-pigeon pea intercrop fails only once in thirty-six years in experiments carried out by the Project on Dryland Farming.

Sustainable agricultural systems integrate crops, livestock and trees. The fodder from crops is food, not 'waste', and the manure from cattle is a source of renewable soil fertility, not 'pollution'. Organic manure and composted green manures, microorganisms such as nitrogen-fixing bacteria, and earthworms increase soil fertility and hence agricultural production, and the increase of organic matter in soil contributes to the conservation of water.

When crops and livestock are separated into distinct product components through agricultural industrialization, they no longer support each other in an integrated system. They become competitors. Crop production strategies that ignore the need for livestock lead to non-sustainable chemical inputs being substituted for sustainable soil fertility renewed with animal wastes. This in turn breaks the cycle of integration between plants and animals on the farm. In a complementary system of agriculture, the cattle eat what the humans cannot. They eat straw from the crops, and grass from pastures and field boundaries. In a competitive model, grain is diverted from human consumption to intensive feed for livestock. It takes 2 kg of grain to produce 1 kg of poultry, 4 kg of grain to produce 1 kg of pork, and 8 kg of grain to produce 1 kg of beef.

The Green Revolution, by destroying diversity in favour of monoculture, as India's experience demonstrates, increases the need for agricultural land. In India 22 per cent of the energy, 3 per cent of the protein and 29 per cent of the organic matter fed to Indian cattle is converted into useful products, compared to 9 per cent, 7 per cent and 5 per cent respectively in the intensive cattle industry in the USA. In terms of conversion of matter and energy, therefore, Indian cattle breeds are three times more efficient than the 'high-productivity' cattle in factory farms (George Shanti, *Operation Food*, 1985). Yet this highly efficient small-farm food system, based on multiple uses of cattle, has been dismantled in the name of efficiency and 'development'. Competition replaces complementarity, linearity replaces cyclical processes, high inputs replace low inputs and single-commodity products replace multi-dimensional uses.

Biodiversity does not only provide sustainable sources for replenishing the fertility of the soil. It is also the most sustainable means of pest control. When diverse crops are grown by farmers, different plants play host to different species, and some of these, like beetles and spiders, are friendly creatures that control pests. Biodiversity creates a pest-predator balance. When pesticides are sprayed, predators are killed, and pest populations explode. Biodiversity is also an important source of safe plant-based pesticides. *Solenium nigrum, Phyllanthus niruri, Pongamia, Pinata, Asatoda vasika, Azadirichta indica, Vitex nigundi* are just some of the plants which offer us safe, effective, sustainable and natural pest control. The revocation of the neem patent in the European Patent Office is a major step in keeping open access to ecological pesticides and fungicides, and preventing these miracles of biodiversity from becoming corporate monopolies.

Biodiversity allows us to practise a peaceful, non-violent agriculture in which there is room for all species, and which increases both sustainability and yields. Conserving biodiversity in agriculture frees farmers from chemical pesticides, herbicides, fertilizers. It frees society from the burden of building large dams for intensive irrigation. It saves resources for individual producers and society. By saving resources it makes them go further – thus ensuring sustainability and equity.

Feeding the Hungry

Food is our most basic need. Agriculture is the domain where one can both metaphorically and materially see how it is possible to have one's cake and eat it. Seeds are sown in the earth. At harvest they yield food and seeds for the next crop – farm-saved seeds – thus maintaining the sustainability and continuity of production.

A myth promoted by the one-dimensional monoculture paradigm is that biodiversity reduces yields and productivity, and monocultures increase yields and productivity. However, since yields and productivity are theoretically constructed terms, they change according to the context. Yields usually refers to production per unit area of a single crop. Planting only one crop in the entire field as a monoculture will of course increase its yield. Planting multiple crops in a mixture will have low yields of individual crops, but will have high total output of food (Shiva, *Biodiversity-based Productivity*, 1996; Rosset and Altieri, 'The Productivity of Small-Scale Agriculture', 1999).

The Mayan peasants in the Chiapas are characterized as unproductive because they produce only 2 tonnes of corn per acre. However, the overall food output is 20 tonnes per acre. In the terraced fields of the high Himalayas, women peasants grow jhangora (barnyard millet), marsha (amaranth), tur (pigeon pea), urad (black gram), gahat (horse gram), soya bean (glysine max), bhat (glysine soya), rayans (rice bean), swanta (cow pea), koda (finger millet) in mixtures and rotations. The total output, even in bad years, approaches 2,450 kg per hectare (13,250 lbs per acre), which is almost six times more than industrially farmed rice monocultures.

The work of the Research Foundation for Science, Technology and Ecology (based in New Delhi) has shown that farm incomes can increase threefold by giving up chemicals and using internal inputs produced by on-farm biodiversity, including straw, animal manure and other by-products. Research done by FAO (the Farming and Agricultural Organization of the UN) has shown that small biodiverse farms can produce thousands of times more food than large, industrial monocultures.

- Indigenous farmers of the Andes grow more than 3,000 varieties of potato.
- In Papua New Guinea, as many as 5,000 varieties of sweet potato are under cultivation, with more than 20 varieties grown in a single garden (Heywood, *Global Biodiversity Assessment*, 1995).
- In Java, small farmers cultivate 607 species in their home gardens, with an overall species diversity comparable to a deciduous tropical forest.
- In sub-Saharan Africa, women cultivate as many as 120 different plants in the spaces left alongside the cash crops.
- A single home garden in Thailand has more than 230 species.
- African home gardens have more than 60 species of trees.
- Rural families in the Congo eat leaves from more than 50 different species of trees.
- A study in eastern Nigeria found that home gardens occupying only 2 per cent of a household's farmland accounted for half of the farm's total output.
- Home gardens in Indonesia are estimated to provide more than 20 per cent of household income and 40 per cent of domestic food supplies (FAO, *Women Feed the World*, 1990).

The main argument used for the industrialization of food and corporatization of agriculture is the low productivity of the small farmer. Surely these families on their little plots of land are incapable of meeting the world's need for food! Industrial agriculture claims that it increases yields, hence creating the image that more food is produced per unit acre by industrial means than by the traditional practices of smallholders. However, sustainable diversified small-farm systems are actually more productive.

Industrial agriculture productivity is high only in the restricted context of a 'part of a part' whether it be the forest or of the farm. For example, 'high-yield' plantations pick one tree species among thousands, for yields of one part of the tree (e.g. woodpulp), whereas traditional forestry practices use many parts of many forest species.

'High-yield' Green Revolution cropping patterns select one crop among hundreds, such as wheat, for the use of just one part, the grain. These high partial yields do not translate into high total yields, because everything else in the farm system goes to waste. Usually the yield of a single crop like wheat or maize is singled out and compared to yields of new varieties. This calculation is biased to make the new varieties appear 'high-yielding' even when, at the systems level, they may not be.

Traditional farming systems are based on mixed and rotational cropping systems of cereals, pulses, and oil seeds with different varieties of each crop, while the Green Revolution package is based on genetically uniform monocultures. No realistic assessments are ever made of the yield of the diverse crop outputs in the mixed and rotational systems.

Productivity is quite different, however, when it is measured in the context of diversity. Biodiversity-based measures of productivity show that small farmers can feed the world. Their multiple yields result in truly high productivity, composed as they are of the multiple yields of diverse species used for diverse purposes. Thus productivity is not lower on smaller units of land: on the contrary, it is higher. In Brazil, the productivity of a farm of up to 10 hectares was $85/hectare while the productivity of a 500-hectare farm was $2 per hectare. In India, a farm of up to 5 acres had a productivity of Rs. 735 per acre, while a 35-acre farm had a productivity of Rs. 346 per acre (Bandopadhyay, 'Food Security and Liberalization', 1996). Comparative studies of 22 rice-growing systems have shown that indigenous systems are more efficient in terms of yields, and also in terms of labour-use and energy-use (Shiva, *The Violence of the Green Revolution*, 1996).

In the Himalayas, peasants have more than 200 species on their farms. They cultivate diverse species in mixtures and rotations, and harvest both cultivated and uncultivated species. In Bengal, women use more than 125 plants, both cultivated and wild, for food. Even the World Development Report (WDR) has accepted that small farms are more productive than large ones. The state of Bengal, after its land reform which turned land back to peasants, was showing a high rate of growth of 6.5 per cent, while the growth rate for India as a whole was a mere 3 per cent (Bandopadhyay).

An article by Francesca Bray in the *Scientific American* ('Agriculture for Developing Nations', July 1994) has developed this approach further, showing how the agricultural productivity calculations of the dominant paradigm distort the real measure of productivity. They leave out the benefits of internal inputs derived from biodiversity. They also neglect to count the additional financial and ecological costs of monoculture industrialization generated by external inputs which substitute for the natural resources of biologically diverse systems.

A study comparing traditional polycultures with industrial monocultures shows that a polyculture system can produce 100 units of food from 5 units of inputs whereas an industrial system requires 300 units of input to produce the same 100 units. The 295 units of wasted inputs could have provided 5,900 units of additional food. Thus the industrial system leads to a decline of 5,900 units of food. This is a recipe for starving people, not for feeding them (Bray, 'Agriculture for Developing Nations').

What does all this evidence mean in terms of 'feeding the world'? It becomes clear that industrial breeding has actually reduced food security by destroying small farms and the small farmers' capacity to produce these diverse outputs of nutritious crops. Both from the point of view of food productivity and food entitlements, industrial agriculture is deficient as compared to diversity-based internal input systems. Protecting small farms which conserve biodiversity is thus a food security imperative.

The polycultures of traditional agricultural systems have evolved because more yield can be harvested from a given area planted with diverse crops than from an equivalent area consisting of separate patches of monocultures. For example, in plantings of sorghum and pigeon pea mixtures, one hectare will produce the same yields as 0.94 hectares of sorghum monoculture and 0.68 hectares of pigeon pea monoculture. Thus one hectare of polyculture produces what 1.62 hectares of monoculture can produce. This is called the land equivalent ratio (LER).

Increased land-use efficiency and higher LER has been reported for polycultures of: millet/groundnut 1.26; maize/bean 1.38; millet/ sorghum 1.53; maize/pigeon pea 1.85; maize/cocoyam/sweet potato 2.08; cassava/maize/groundnut >2.51. (Rosset and Altieri, 'The Productivity of Small-Scale Agriculture', 1999.) The monocultures of the Green Revolution thus actually reduced food yields per acre previously achieved through mixtures of diverse crops. This falsifies the argument often made that chemically intensive agriculture and genetic engineering will save biodiversity by releasing land from food production. In fact, since monocultures require more land, biodiversity is destroyed twice over – once on the farm, and then on the additional acreage required to produce the outputs a monoculture has displaced.

As Jules Pretty reports in *Feeding the World* (Action Aid, 1999):

- 100,000 farmers in Benin have increased yields using mucuna bean as a green manure and cover crop with maize to suppress weeds and fix nitrogen.
- 45,000 farmers in Guatemala and Honduras have used regenerative techniques to triple maize yields from 400–600 kg per hectare to 2–2.5 tonnes per hectare.
- 300,000 farmers in dryland India, using water and soil conservation techniques, have tripled sorghum and millet yields to 2–2.5 tonnes per hectare.
- 12,500 farmers in Ethiopia have improved their nutrition level by 70 per cent and crop yields by 60 per cent by using organic methods.
- 9 million hectares in southern Brazil have shifted to sustainable agriculture. Maize yields have risen from 3 to 5 tonnes per hectare and soya bean yields from 2.8 to 4.7 tonnes per hectare.

Data shows that, everywhere in the world, biodiverse small farms produce more agricultural output per unit area than large farms. Even in the USA, small farms of 27 acres or less have 10 times greater dollar output per acre than larger farms (Rosset and Altieri, 'The Productivity of Small-Scale Agriculture'). It is therefore time to switch from measuring monoculture yields to assessing biodiversity outputs in farming systems.

Thus both at the level of individual peasant farms and at national level, the Green Revolution has led to a decline in food security. The same applies to the Gene Revolution. What the Green Revolution achieved was an increase in industrial inputs, which, of course, created growth for the agrichemical and fossil-fuel industry. But this increased consumption of toxins and energy by the agricultural sector did not translate into more food.

Today, most of the 830 million people who lack adequate access to food are rural communities whose entitlements have collapsed either due to environmental degradation or due to livelihood destruction and negative terms of trade. Food security is therefore intimately connected to the livelihood security of small rural producers. There are proven alternatives to industrial agriculture and genetic engineering, and these are based on small farms and ecological methods. Sound resource-use combined with social justice is the path of sustainability in agriculture that we should be taking.

Across the world, initiatives that free agriculture of industrial inputs are showing that both food production and farmers' incomes can increase by shifting to ecological agriculture:

- In Indonesia, restrictions were introduced on the use of 57 pesticides in rice-growing, and subsidies for pesticides were eliminated. From 1987 to 1990, the volume of pesticides used on rice fell by over 50 per cent, while yields increased by about 15 per cent. Farmers' net incomes increased by $18 per farmer per season. The government save $120 million per year by ending pesticide subsidies.
(Thrupp, 'New Partnerships for Sustainable Agriculture', 1997.)
- In Bangladesh the 'No Pest' programme led to pesticide reduction

of 76 per cent and yield increases of 11 per cent. Returns increased by an average of 106 per cent in the dry season and 26 per cent in the wet season. (Thrupp.)

- In Peru, ecological agriculture has contributed to a net benefit of $162 per hectare, $70 from yield increase and $92 from reduced costs of inputs. With wider diffusion, net benefit could reach $288, $183 from yield increase and $105 from cost savings. (UNDP, *Agroecology*, 1995.)
- The UNDP project on sustainable agriculture reports tripling and quadrupling of yields from 400 kg per hectare to 1,200 to 1,600 kg per hectare in Honduras, and potato yield going up to 8–14 kg per hectare per year The project was based on the indigenous Waru-Waru system of raised fields evolved in the high plains of the Peruvian Andes. (Thrupp.)
- A review of sustainable-agriculture projects in 20 countries covering 1.93 million households shows that yields of wheat, maize and sorghum doubled when farmers shifted from high external-input agriculture to biodiversity-based agriculture using low external inputs. (Thrupp.)

To assess the real productivity of a farming system from the perspective of the farmer and of the soil we need to measure the biodiversity-based productivity. We also need to calculate:

1 The value of diverse outputs from diverse species and their diverse functions.
2 The value of internal inputs provided by diverse farm outputs (e.g. straw for organic manure).
3 The costs of purchased inputs, such as fertilizers, pesticides, herbicides.
4 The ecological costs of external chemical inputs.

The higher productivity of diversity-based systems indicates that there is an alternative to genetic engineering and industrial agriculture – an alternative that is more ecological and more equitable. This alternative is based on the intensification of biodiversity – intensifying through integrating diverse species – in place of chemical intensification, which promotes monocultures and, unlike its ecological alternative, fails to take all outputs of all species into account.

The Survival of Small Farmers

All around the world, food production has been transformed into a negative economy as farmers spend ever increasing amounts on purchasing inputs and receive decreasing prices for their produce. Low farm prices are usually explained as being a result of surpluses and overproduction. However, low prices are more closely linked to monocultures and monopolies. When all farmers grow only one commodity, there will of course be a surplus of that one product. But this is a pseudo-surplus, not a real surplus. It is not the surplus left after nature's needs for ecological maintenance have been met, and also the farm's family needs for food and sustenance. The destruction of biodiversity in industrial agricultural systems means that all the functions that biodiversity could perform for the farmer at no cost have to be bought. Given the vertical integration of agriculture and food production, the same agribusiness corporations sell external inputs to the farmer and buy farmers' produce. In developed countries, only 15 per cent of the price of a loaf of bread goes to the farmer – the rest goes on milling, baking, packaging, transport and marketing. For agribusiness high production costs and low commodity prices translate into two-way profits. For the farmer, they translate into a negative economy and spiralling debts.

Farmers everywhere are being paid a fraction of what they received for the same commodity a decade ago. In the USA wheat prices at the farm dropped from $5.75 a bushel to $2.43, soya bean prices dropped from $8.40 to $4.2 and corn prices dropped from $4.43 to $1.72. In India, from 1999 to 2000, prices for coffee dropped from Rs. 60 to Rs. 18 per kg, and prices of oilseed declined by more than 30 per cent.

The Canadian National Farmers Union put it like this to the Senate in a report called 'The Farm Crisis', 18 February 2000:

> While the farmers growing cereal grains – wheat, oats, corn – earn negative returns and are pushed close to bankruptcy, the companies that make breakfast cereals reap huge profits. In 1998, cereal companies Kellogg's, Quaker Oats, and General Mills enjoyed return on equity rates of 56 per cent, 165 per cent and 222 per cent

respectively. While a bushel of corn sold for less than $4, a bushel of corn flakes sold for $133. In 1998, the cereal companies were 186 to 740 times more profitable than the farms. Maybe farmers are making too little because others are taking too much.

A false logic is often established according to which industrial agriculture produces more food, and increased production leads to lower prices. When viewed in terms of total food output, industrial agriculture does not produce more nutrition, and low prices are connected to monopoly control, not to productivity. Further, the so-called surpluses are in reality pseudo-surpluses because they are based on taking nutrition out of the soil without returning food for the soil-food web. They are also pseudo-surpluses because they are based on taking food away from food-producers who starve even as markets are saturated. They are pseudo-surpluses because they deny producers a fair share of the price. Finally, they are not real surpluses because imports and exports camouflage real production at national level, giving the illusion of surpluses.

How fictitious 'surpluses' created by free trade can be is well illustrated in the case of wheat in India. Trade liberalization is supposed to bring benefits to national agricultural economies. However, the beneficiaries are neither the farmers nor the governments of the Third World. A recent editorial of a business daily in India ran the headline 'Freeing Wheat'. It is significant to ask from what wheat is being freed and for whom it is being freed. Wheat needs to be freed from chemicals, and wheat farmers need to be freed from their bondage to chemical and seed corporations. However, the reference is to the freedom of corporations and grain-traders. The freedom to export food grain under liberalized trade has already benefited the giant grain traders, Cargill and Continental. They bought wheat at $60 to $100 per tonne from India and sold it at $230–40 per tonne in the international market in 1996, making a profit of $130–70 per tonne, while India lost $100m in exports because of the concentration of power in the hands of five grain merchants. The US grain giants turned to the Indian market because the large-scale wheat monocultures in the

USA, the bread-basket of the world, had been affected in nearly 50 per cent of the farmland by a combination of drought and a fungal disease. As a result of the US crop failure, India's wheat exports increased dramatically.

Exports of wheat, however, led to domestic shortages and a rise in prices. The two million tonnes that were exported in mid-1996, were in effect re-imported in late 1996 to overcome domestic shortages. Agricultural growth did take place, but not in terms of food and not for India. The quantity of wheat in the world and in India remained the same, India's foreign exchange expenditure increased, leaving India financially poorer. Because of a domestic price increase there was a decrease in the food entitlements of the poor. Only the 'Merchants of Grain' gained from the liberalization of wheat exports and imports.

The so-called oceans of milk and mountains of butter in Europe are not absolute surpluses but surpluses resulting from imports. As Tracy Worcester points out in *Resurgence* (March/April 2000):

In 1996, Britain exported 111 million litres of milk and imported 173 million litres. It imported 49 million kilograms of butter, but it exported 47 million. Why didn't it just consume its own 47 million kilos and import the shortfall of 2 million, thus saving all the transportation costs? Why? Because not importing and exporting on a grand scale produces no profits for the transnational and their transport fleets. The food giants will fly apples to Britain from 14,000 miles away in New Zealand and bring green beans 4,000 miles from Kenya, although British farmers can easily grow both.

Pseudo-productivity based on a faulty monocultural assessment, combined with pseudo-surpluses based on flawed rules of economic globalization does create growth for agribusiness, but is pushing farmers everywhere into debt, displacement and destitution.

The epidemic of farmers' suicides in India is the most dramatic impact of trade liberalization in agriculture. India is the home of cotton. Gandhi transformed the spinning-wheel into the symbol of Indian's freedom from British colonialism. But under conditions of globalization, cotton has become a symbol of a new bondage. Globalization led to increased exports. Increased cotton exports led to increased cotton cultivation, including expansion into semi-arid areas such as Warangal in Andhra Pradesh where farmers earlier grew food crops for subsistence. Warangal has not traditionally been an area for cotton cultivation. In this predominantly food-crop area, cotton is a relatively new crop, introduced under trade liberalization. Under corporate persuasion, farmers of Warangal switched over from their traditional paddy (rice), pulses, millets, oilseeds and vegetable crops, which had sustained them, to the sowing of cotton. Seed companies used video vans to show films selling hybrid cotton seed, promising that it would make them millionaires. Hybrid seed was sold as 'White Gold'. However, instead of becoming millionaires, the poor peasants were driven into a debt bondage from which they could free themselves only though suicide.

In Warangal thirty years ago, the total acreage under cotton crop was negligible. According to the available data, in 1986–87 it was nearly 33,000 hectares (or approximately 82,000 acres), which increased to 100,600 hectares (or 250,000 acres) in 1996–97, an increase of nearly 300 per cent in one decade. The cultivation of cotton has basically replaced food crops like jowar and sorghum. In 1986–87 the area under jowar was almost 78,000 hectares (192,500 acres); in 1996–97 this went down to 27,300 hectares (67,400 acres). The acreage under the traditional paddy and under bajra (millet) has also decreased in the last 10 years. In 1986–87, total land under bajra was nearly 11,300 hectares (27,900 acres) which has been drastically reduced to 400 hectares (just under 1,000 acres) in 1996–97.

Under the pressures of globalization, not only did cultivation shift from food to export crops, and from mixed and diverse farming to monocultures, liberalization had also led to a shift in seed supply from the farmers' seed, and public-sector seed to seed from private corporations. The new atmosphere of market liberalization implied a withdrawal of regulatory systems in the seed sector. Companies could sell what they want and claim what they want without any system of social and public accountability. Untested and untried seeds were sold at high prices to gullible and innocent peasants with no experience of dealing with corporate salesmen, and whose local knowledge has been displaced by corporate advertising. Under corporate pressure, unleashed by privatization and globalization, seeds also changed from openly pollinated indigenous varieties, saved by farmers and adapted to local conditions, to hybrids, purchased every year at high cost and ecologically vulnerable. Hybrids mean more profits for corporations, but higher costs for peasants and the environment.

Since monocultures and hybrids are very vulnerable to pest attacks, pesticide use also increased. Pesticide use in the district went up from $2.5 million in the 1980s to $50m in 1997, a 2,000 per cent increase over a decade. Pesticides are chemicals, and they have unleashed a war against nature on our farms and fields. Beneficial species have been wiped out, increasing pest problems since without predators pests flourish. The more the pests increase in this war against nature, the more the peasants spray poisons. For poor peasants, this cost can only be borne through debts (Shiva and Jafri, *Seeds of Suicide*, 1998).

Since trade liberalization has also led to budget cutbacks on extension services, the closing-down of cooperatives and public-sector banks, which provided rural credit at low interest, the peasants had to take high-interest credit from the same companies that were selling hybrid seeds and pesticides. The corporations thus became moneylenders, extension agents, seed suppliers and pesticide salesmen all rolled into one. The peasants were soon buried under the weight of unpayable debt. In 1998, more than 500 farmers committed suicide in Warangal district alone. The suicides continued in 1999. Across India, over 20,000 peasants have committed suicide since 1998. Liberalization of exports combined with liberalization of the seed sector and liberalization of credit has been responsible for the death of peasants in India, the destruction of biodiversity and the poisoning of agro-ecosystems. Globalization has removed all protection from farmers and from nature.

In the regions where the high costs of hybrid seeds and industrial agriculture introduced through globalization are already pushing farmers to suicide, Monsanto has now introduced its genetically engineered cotton seeds. Most of the big Indian seed companies such as MAHYCO, Parry, Rallis, have already been bought up by Monsanto. While the argument used to promote genetically engineered crops in the Third World is that they will increase yields and decrease pesticides, the trials showed a decrease in yields and an increase in the use of pesticides (Shiva, Jafri and Emani, 'Globalization and the Threat to Seed Security', 1999). If India were to adopt the Monsanto model, it is feared that more farmers might fall into debt, more species might disappear and more superpests might emerge. That is why on 9 August 1998, the anniversary of the day that Gandhi told the British to 'Quit India', we started the 'Monsanto, Quit India' movement. Farmers in Andhra Pradesh and Karnataka uprooted the genetically engineered cotton in protest, and we have filed a case in the Supreme Court to stop the introduction of genetically engineered crops in Indian agriculture. The Third World does not need genetic engineering in agriculture. Genetic engineering introduces new ecological risks and new economic costs which the Third World peasants cannot afford (Supreme Court Case, RFSTE, Writ Petition No. 71,1999).

Biodiversity-based agriculture protects the earth as well as the farmers. It is based on genuine surpluses with produce traded only after the needs of the earth, other species, and local households and communities have been met. Ecological security, nutritional security and livelihood security therefore converge instead of being in conflict. The conservation of biodiversity and the shift to sustainable practices based on internal inputs from the farm is not only good for the planet. It is also the only way farmers can escape from the vicious circle of debt and a negative economy. Organic farming is growing everywhere, because consumers do not want to be poisoned with toxic residues from agrichemicals. But organic agriculture is also necessary from the point of view of small producers.

The International Federation of Organic Agriculture Movements (IFOAM) is the international platform for strengthening organic agriculture. In India, ARISE and Navdanya are spearheading the organic movement. The Rodale Institute in USA and the Soil Association in the UK have played pioneering roles in making organic agriculture a reality. Interestingly, both organizations were inspired by Sir Albert Howard, who was sent to India in 1905 as the Imperial Economic Botanist, but gave up the chemical methods he had been sent to spread. Instead, he learnt organic methods from Indian peasants, did a reverse transfer of technology, and came to be known as the father of modern organic agriculture. Howard identified diversity as the basic difference between sustainable agriculture as practised by the peasants in India and non-sustainable industrial agriculture.

> The main characteristic of Nature's farming can therefore be summed up in a few words. Mother Earth never attempts to farm without livestock; she always raises mixed crops; great pains are taken to preserve the soil and to prevent erosion; the mixed vegetable and animal waste are converted into humus; there is no waste; the processes of growth and the processes of decay balance one another; ample provision is made to maintain large reserves of fertility; the greatest care is taken to store the rainfall; both plants and animals are left to protect themselves against disease. The agriculture practices of the Orient have passed the supreme test – they are almost as permanent as those of the primeval forest, of the prairie or of the ocean. The smallholdings of China, for example, are still maintaining a steady output and there is no loss of fertility after forty centuries of management.

We can have our cake and eat it too – to the extent that we return to nature what we take from her, and we return to the producers a fair share of the produce they gift to us. This is what the growing movement of organic agriculture and fair trade embodies.

Sustainability and Equity

Sustainability in agriculture has two dimensions: natural resource sustainability and socio-economic sustainability.

Natural resource sustainability is based on the stability of the agricultural ecosystems based on interactions between soil, water and biodiversity. This sustainability measures the wealth of 'nature's economy' and the foundation of all other economies. Nature's economy includes biodiversity, soil fertility and soil- and water-conservation; this provides the ecological capital for agriculture.

Socio-economic sustainability relates to the social ecology of agriculture, including the relationship of society to the environment, the relationship between different social groups engaged in agricultural production, and the relationship between producers and consumers which is invariably mediated by traders, government agencies and corporations. Socio-economic sustainability measures the health of the 'people's economy', or the economy of sustenance, in which human needs of livelihoods and nutrition are met. The people's economy includes the diverse costs and benefits, both material and financial, that farming communities derive from agriculture.

There are quite clearly two different meanings of 'sustainability'. The true meaning refers to nature's and people's sustainability. It involves a recovery of the recognition that nature supports our lives and livelihoods – it is the primary source of sustenance. It implies maintaining the integrity of nature's processes, cycles and rhythms. There is a second kind of 'sustainability', which refers to the market. It involves maintaining supplies of raw material for industrial production and long-distance global consumption. Markets grow while soils and rural communities are impoverished. This is the conventional definition of 'conservation' – making available sustained yields of raw material for development. And since industrial raw materials and market commodities have substitutes, sustainability is translated into substitutability of materials, which is further translated into convertibility into profits and cash.

Both environmental and social sustainability have been undermined because nature's economy and the people's economy have been neglected and eroded by the dominant paradigm of economic development, which only recognizes the market economy, and only measures growth in the market economy, even though this growth is often associated with the destruction and shrinkage of nature's economy and the people's economy. The ecological base of agriculture has been destroyed and farmers face large-scale displacement.

Sustainability in nature involves the regeneration of nature's processes and a subservience to nature's laws of return. Sustainability of agricultural communities involves the regeneration and revitalization of the culture and local economy of agricultural production. Sustainability in the marketplace involves ensuring the supplies of raw material, the flow of commodities, the accumulation of capital, and returns on investment. It cannot provide the sustenance that we are losing by impairing nature's capacities to support life. The growth of global markets also hides the destruction of the local economy of domestic production and consumption.

The transition to sustainable agriculture requires that the two neglected economies of nature and people should be included in the assessment of productivity and cost-benefit analysis in agriculture. Development and economic growth are perceived exclusively in terms of processes of capital accumulation. However, the growth of financial resources in the market economy often takes place by diverting natural resources from the people's survival economy, and nature's economy. On the one hand, this generates conflicts over natural resources: on the other hand, it creates an ecologically unstable constellation of nature, people and capital.

A system of productivity-assessment is therefore needed that reflects the full costs and full benefits of agricultural systems, and measures the maintenance, growth and destruction in the three economies of nature, people and the market, not merely the growth in the market economy from the perspective of dominant commercial interests. Reflection of the full range of goods and services requires that the 'productivity' and 'yield' should be based on a calculation of diversity, and not on a reductionist category of a part of the agricultural system.

The modernization of forestry, fishing technology, agriculture and animal husbandry destroys many species and breeds, and favours factory farming. Basing productivity-increase on the destruction of diversity is dangerous and unnecessary. Monocultures are ecologically and socially non-sustainable – they destroy both nature's economy and the people's economy.

Not until diversity is made the logic of productivity can diversity be conserved. 'Improvement' from the corporate viewpoint, or from the viewpoint of Western agricultural or forestry research, is often a loss for the Third World, especially for the poor in the Third World.

Plant-improvement in agriculture has been based on the 'enhancement' of the yield of the desired product at the expense of unwanted plant parts. The 'desired' product is, however, not the same for agribusiness and Third World peasants. The parts of a farming system that will be treated as 'unwanted' depends on one's class and gender. 'Development,' by squeezing out those aspects of biodiversity that agribusiness does not want, fosters poverty and ecological decline.

Overall productivity and sustainability is much higher in mixed systems of farming and forestry. Taking diversity into account leads to sound resource-use and to sound science. Through the maintenance of the complex interactions between the different elements of farming systems and through the conservation of ecological processes that renew soil fertility, moisture and biodiversity, agricultural production can be made sustainable. It is only the sustainable systems that will be able to feed the world in the future.

CHAPTER 5

THE FUTURE OF BIODIVERSITY

In the words of the poet Goethe in his *Scientific Studies*, 'We conceive of the individual animal as a small world, existing for its own sake, by its own means. Every creature has its own reason to be. All its parts have a direct effect on one another, a relationship to one another, thereby constantly reviewing the circle of life.'

The future of biodiversity is in our hands. The more ecological space we leave for other species, the more economic space we leave for the marginalized sectors of society – peasants, women and children – and for future generations to meet their needs. Biodiversity is therefore not just an indicator of sustainability, it is also an indicator of justice. Compassion for other species translates into compassion for our fellow humans. If we can protect the earthworm, the butterfly and the bee, we will also protect our small farmers, because the same technological and trade structures that push butterflies and bees to extinction are pushing small farmers everywhere to extinction.

The protection of biodiversity demands some radical shifts in our thinking, in our consumption and production patterns, and in our policies in order to protect the millions of other species which have as much right to live and survive as human beings. And the industrialized West will have to make even more radical changes because it is even more deeply entrenched in ways of thought and ways of life that squeeze out diverse species and their diverse functions.

The conservation of biodiversity offers us an opportunity to undo two basic colonizations – the colonization of nature and the colonization of other cultures. This demands changes at very fundamental levels – in the dominant worldview, in approaches to science and technology, in concepts of 'wealth' and 'property'. The 'empty earth' paradigm leads to the denial of prior inhabitants and their prior rights, and to the notion that there are no ecological, cultural or ethical limits. It also creates a divided world – divisions which exist and deepen even in globalization, and were evident in the failed round of the WTO talks in Seattle in 1999. The 'full land' concept makes us recognize that every step we take is in a world populated by a tremendous variety of species and cultures. It allows us to recognize ecological limits set by the basic rights of diverse species to exist. Sustainability and democracy are both built on respecting limits set by others' rights. In an age of globalization and biotechnology, the recognition of these limits becomes even more significant, since globalization and genetic engineering maximize exploitation and profits by erasing limits and boundaries.

The Genetic Mine paradigm based on the idea of 'empty life' is today's 'empty earth' equivalent since it empties biodiversity of the creative contributions of nature and other cultures. In Hindi, the words *vasudhiv kutumbam* mean 'Earth Family', the democracy of all life, from tiny to huge – all have a part in holding the web of life together.

Changing Knowledge Systems

Technology has become a major arena of conflict related to biodiversity. During the Green Revolution, no value was given to biodiversity and there was no concern for the cost of its destruction or the need for its conservation. The resistance to genetic engineering in agriculture is in large measure rooted in the threat it poses to biodiversity, either by the spread of herbicide-resistant crops which leads to the destruction of all except the commercial crop itself, or by the spread of genetic pollution and genetic contamination. The Monarch butterfly and the honey-bee have become important prisms for the assessment of biotechnology .

The ordinary citizen has begun to think of concern for other species as an important part of being fully human, but the biotech industry, technocrats, and in some cases politicians are stuck in a discourse that has lost resonance with citizens. This gap in perceptions, values, and worldviews is especially evident in debates related to genetic engineering. People are impatient for a paradigm change. Industry, however, clings to an outmoded mechanistic paradigm to promote its new biotechnologies.

Acknowledging other species requires thinking based on interrelationships, complexity diversity and self-organization. These paradigms are already emerging in the sciences but must become the basis of technology and trade. Progress in technology and growth in economics have been predicated on biodiversity destruction. Our concepts of technological and economic progress and efficiency need to undergo rapid and radical change on the basis of biodiversity conservation.

Reductionism destroys biodiversity because it reduces our complex, diverse and dynamic world into a fragmented, atomized and uniform construction. This atomization and uniformity in turn lead to the insensitive manipulation of ecosystems and species to increase partial and fragmented production. This creates an illusion of surplus, which is in reality scarcity because it takes from nature and nature's species more than is ecologically sustainable, and from the poor their rightful share in the gifts of biodiversity.

Industrial farming, industrial fisheries, industrial forestry and industrial medicine have all been shaped by this reductionist worldview. It has also destroyed cultural diversity because non-reductionist systems of indigenous knowledge have been discounted and discarded as unscientific.

A shift in the paradigm of knowledge from a reductionist to a relational approach is necessary for the protection of both biological diversity and cultural diversity. A relational view of living systems recognizes the intrinsic worth of all species, protects their ecological space and respects their self-organizational, diverse, dynamic and evolving capacities. It creates the possibility of a multiplicity of knowledge systems to include indigenous and traditional knowledge systems as well as modern systems of ecological approaches to biology.

Genetic engineering is based on genetic reductionism. This in turn leads to properties being treated as if they are 'created', even though they already exist in nature and other cultures. The salinity-resistance and drought-resistance in crops already exist through millennia of nature's evolution and human selection. Proteins and vitamins occur naturally in plants. Putting amaranth genes or beta-carotene genes into rice does not 'create' protein or beta-carotene, it relocates it. The prior existence of these traits is ignored, as is the impact of relocation of genes on biodiversity. Benefits are thus exaggerated, and costs negated. The destruction is defined as inevitable and necessary – otherwise, we are told, there will be no food or medicine.

Scientists around the world are challenging the dominant paradigm of genetic reductionism, and evolving a science based on gene- ecology. They show that the leap from DNA to complex functions like intelligence, disease states and psychological states is unjustified. Complex, self-organizing, dynamic living systems are not reducible only to constituent genes. Sciences of processes are replacing the reductionist science of mechanics and objects, sciences of qualities are replacing the science of Cartesian quantity. However, as natural science moves into ecological and context-dependent paradigms consistent with diversity, technology is moving into a crude, mechanical paradigm based on competition rather than cooperation, monocultures rather than diversity, control rather than self-organization.

The future of biodiversity will be shaped by our capacity to evolve technologies that respect biodiversity and the intrinsic worth of all species and their relationships, and to assess the impact of reductionist technologies like genetic engineering on biodiversity and ecosystems. This is why the Biosafety Protocol is vital. Tomorrow's biodiversity will also be shaped by the capacity of the dominant Western culture to recognize the value of indigenous knowledge systems for the sustainable use of biodiversity. This is why the debates on the patenting of life forms and indigenous knowledge are so crucial both for the future of indigenous cultures and the biodiversity which has shaped them.

Changing Concepts of Wealth and Property

The conservation of biodiversity can only be ensured through a world view that recognizes the intrinsic worth of all species, and does not assess the value of a species only as industrial raw material. Simple justice also demands such a change in concepts of value, since two-thirds of humanity live in an economy based on biodiversity. When monocultures of export crops replace food crops, local people go hungry. When herbicides wipe out biodiversity, the poor – and women are the most numerous of the world's poor – are deprived of food, cattle fodder and medicine. Whenever we engage in consumption or production patterns which take more than we need, we are engaging in a violent economic order. According to an ancient Indian text, the *Isopanishad*: 'A selfish man over-utilizing the resources of nature to satisfy his own ever increasing needs is nothing but a thief, because using resources beyond one's needs would result in the utilization of resources over which others have a right.' This relationship between restraint in the use of resources and social justice was also the core element of Mahatma Gandhi's political philosophy. In his view: 'The earth provides enough for everyone's needs, but not for everyone's greed.'

The Eurocentric concept of property sees only capital investments as investment, and hence treats returns on capital investment as the only right that needs protection. Non-Western indigenous communities and cultures recognize that investment can also be of labour or of care and nurturance. Rights in such cultural systems protect investments beyond capital. They protect the culture of conservation and the culture of caring and sharing.

Non-violence or *ahimsa* combines justice and sustainability at a deep level. 'Not taking more than you need' ensures that enough resources are left in the ecosystem for other species and that sustainability is maintained by preserving essential ecological processes. It also ensures that resources are left for the diverse needs of different groups of people. The criterion of not taking more than you need is not merely an ethical criterion, it is also the highest expression of the Precautionary Principle, since it avoids harm when we lack full knowledge of the potential impact of our actions. Diversity and pluralism are necessary characteristics of an *ahimsa* or non-violent economic order. If the principle of not encroaching on others' rights is fully followed, diverse species will survive and diverse trades and occupations will also flourish. Diversity is therefore the litmus test for non-violence, and reflects the sustainability and justice that non-violence embodies.

The 'full-life' paradigm prevents theft from others as a way of generating wealth, but it also produces a more fulfilling and satisfying form of wealth and wellbeing for oneself. 'If we imagine that the fullness we yearn for can be reckoned in dollars.... Or purchased in stores, there will be no end to our craving.'(Sanders, *Audubon Society Newsletter*, July/August 1998.)

Biopiracy – the piracy of the knowledge and resources of the poor by the rich – is based on the empty-life worldview which denies nature's creativity and that of other cultures. The 1980 decision of the US Patent Office to grant a patent for a microorganism marked a major ethical shift. It redefined living organisms as human inventions and intellectual property, thus robbing them of their intrinsic worth and their self-organizational capacity. This ethical departure was neither publicly debated nor democratically arrived at. On the other hand, it has been globalized through another undemocratic structure, the WTO and its Trade Related Intellectual Property Rights Agreement. If biopiracy continues, and only the intellectual property rights of scientists and corporations are recognized while the innovations of indigenous people and traditional societies are not, the poor will keep getting poorer as their resources and knowledge are appropriated and privatized.

The culturally biased and narrow notions of rights and property that have shaped Intellectual Property Rights are inappropriate for indigenous cultures, and inadequate for conserving biodiversity and cultural diversity. Through IPRs and TRIPs, a particular Eurocentric culture has been universalized and globalized. When applied to biodiversity, such narrow concepts of rights are mechanisms for denying the intrinsic worth of species, and the prior rights of indigenous communities. Judicial innovation is therefore needed to:

- Protect the biodiversity and cultural integrity of indigenous
  communities, and allow them to continue to use their resources

and knowledge freely as they have done from time immemorial.

• Prevent the piracy and privatization of indigenous biodiversity and indigenous knowledge through IPRs, nationally and internationally.

• Define a public domain of commons in the area of biodiversity and knowledge.

We call these rights 'community intellectual rights' (CIRs) to reflect the collective and communal nature of the innovation and the utilization of indigenous biodiversity. The IPR systems that evolved in industrialized countries as reflected in the TRIPs agreement recognize only Western knowledge systems as scientific and formal, and see non-Western knowledge systems as unscientific and informal.

The creation of monopoly rights in the utilization of biodiversity could have serious implications for national and community rights to biodiversity and indigenous knowledge. TRIPs give countries the option of formulating their own *sui generis* (self-standing) regime for plants as an alternative to patent protection. Collective rights can be a strong candidate for such *sui generis* systems for agricultural and medicinal-plant biodiversity. Therefore, it is crucial that biodiversity-knowledge systems are accorded legal recognition as the common property of the communities concerned. Building such an alternative is essential to prevent the monopoly of biodiversity and knowledge by an unbalanced mechanistic implementation of TRIPs.

There are as yet no binding legal instruments or standards that adequately grant rights to indigenous people's collective knowledge and innovations, thereby protecting their knowledge from biopiracy. That is not to say there is no scope for such developments. On the contrary, trends and precedents in international indigenous rights legislation and case law signify a strong movement in this direction, with several significant judgments being passed in recent years. Further, movements towards ethical and ecological consumption are also creating a new basis for consumption that does not cause ecological destruction or lead to economic deprivation of the poor.

In India, a grassroots movement of village communities – the movement for living democracy – asserts the sovereign duties and rights of local communities to protect biodiversity and use it sustainably in accordance with local culture and conservation values. Beginning with 200 villages in the high Himalaya, on World Environment Day, 5 June 1999, the movement has spread to more than 1,000 villages in different regions. Village communities organized as living democracies – 'Jaiv Panchayats' – are reasserting their duty to defend biodiversity as a commons and their right to generate livelihoods in creative partnership with diverse species. Movements against the patenting of biodiversity and indigenous knowledge are not just about human rights, they are creating an inclusive democracy of human responsibility to protect all beings. As the statement from the 200 villages which launched the Jaiv Panchayat movement proclaimed:

> From our forefathers we have inherited the right to protect the biodiversity of our Himalayan region and also the corresponding duty to utilize these biological resources for the good of all people. Therefore we pledge, by way of this declaration, that we shall not let any destructive elements unjustly exploit and monopolize these precious resources through illegal means. So that in our communities and country we can truly establish a living people's democracy wherein each and every individual can associate herself/himself with the conservation, sustainable and just use of these biological resources in her/his everyday practical living. This tradition of sharing shall be kept alive through the 'Jaiv Panchayat'– the living democracy. The Jaiv Panchayat will decide on all matters pertaining to biodiversity. Through such centralized democratic decision-making we will make real the democracy for life.
>
> Cows, buffaloes, goats, sheep, lions, tigers and in fact all animals, birds, plants, trees, precious medicinal plants and manure, water, soil, seeds are all our biological resources and we shall not let any outsider exercise any control over them through patents or destroy them through genetic engineering.

The living democracy movement retains and deepens democracy at three levels. Firstly, unlike representative democracy which is losing its power to represent the people's will in the face of corporate power, living democracy is dynamic and vibrant – it is alive, not atrophied. Secondly, living democracy centres on matters of life and survival, on every issue of hunger and disease, food and health, not on power for profits. Finally, the living democracy movement includes all life in its embrace. It is about the freedom and rights of *all* species.

Changing the Rules of Trade and Patterns of Consumption

The right to consume anything from anywhere, totally ignoring the true cost, has been redefined as the new concept of freedom in a free-trade context. However, such freedom is based on taking away the freedom of millions of people and millions of species to survive with integrity, dignity and wellbeing. Further, trade agreements like GATT and the WTO ensure that consumers cannot make ethical choices between biodiversity-destroying and biodiversity-conserving production. Such distinctions are made illegal through the concept of a 'like product' which assumes that how a thing is made cannot be the basis of treating products differently in trade. Such a distinction is in fact treated as discriminatory and a trade barrier. However, unless consumers can know which products destroy the ecological space of other species and which do not, consumption patterns cannot become conserving patterns.

The 'battle of Seattle' at the WTO talks in November 1999 was a people's rebellion. It arose from the refusal to sacrifice people's lives and values for corporate profits and greed. It was also a rebellion of Third World governments and European Ministers for the Environment who refused to allow themselves to be marginalized.

Free trade cannot set the rules for our relationships with other species and the rights of people to these biodiversity-based livelihoods and lifestyles. Free-trade rules must change to allow all species and all cultures to flourish. The twenty-first century has to be a biodiversity century: rules of competition must give way to the principle of compassion; the culture of greed and consumerism has to give way to the culture of conservation; the culture of domination needs to give way to the culture of protection; the culture of appropriation must give way to that of sharing and caring.

The lesson to be learnt from biodiversity is cooperation, not competition – the large depends on the small, and cannot survive by exterminating the small. This inclusive freedom shows the way to the future of biodiversity. WTO rules of free trade are threatening biodiversity by expanding monocultures, creating monopolies of ownership and control over the planet's biological wealth and depriving the poor of basic resources. WTO rules are also undermining such multilateral environmental agreements as the CBD. A society in which the corporations have rights at the expense of the citizens' rights is not a free society. It is corporate totalitarianism created through free-trade arrangements. When José Bové and French farmers attacked McDonald's in Millau in response to the WTO ruling forcing Europe to import US beef raised on growth-hormones, they were resisting both McDonald's global influence on eating habits and the rules of WTO. I was invited as an expert witness to the trial on 30 June and 1 July 2000. More than 130,000 people had gathered in this remote village of France to support the French farmers.

Economies in which most people are rendered dispensable, and in which most people cannot meet their basic needs are free economies only in the sense that they are free for capital. Building free societies and free economies means, above all, putting people and nature before capital. The liberation of people and nature is a very different issue from the liberalization of trade.

The future of biodiversity will be intimately associated with the future of humanity. When the Berlin Wall fell, Francis Fukuyama talked of the End of History. However, the protests at Seattle and Washington have made it quite clear that history has not ended, the human future is not foreclosed, and diverse possibilities exist for the future of biodiversity. We will witness an intense contest between two visions of the future: one based on profits and monopolies, the other on compassion and sharing; one based on monocultures, the other on diversity; one based on reductionist science, the other on dynamic complexity; one based on environmentally irresponsible deployment of new technologies by unaccountable corporations, the other based on biosafety and democracy.

Around the world, revolutionary changes are taking place as people recognize the value and worth of biodiversity and reverse the trends that have been pushing species to extinction. A few years ago no one thought twice about letting crop diversity disappear. Today, groups both in the North and South are conserving varieties, setting up seed banks, and reintroducing biodiversity in agriculture. The Rodale Research Institute in the US, and the Henry Doubleday Foundation in the UK have played a pioneering role in the conservation of biodiversity.

In India, I started Navdanya, the seed-savers movement, more than a decade ago. Since then we have helped establish eleven community seed banks in seven states. The shift from costly seeds and chemicals to farm-saved seeds and internal inputs has promoted sustainable agriculture and improved farmers' income. In places like Warangal in Andhra Pradesh and Bhatinda in Punjab where the debts due to high-cost seeds and pesticides have pushed farmers to suicide, Navdanya seed banks are spreading seeds of hope, helping farmers off the chemical treadmill and out of a vicious circle of a despair. In coastal Orissa, a super cyclone in October 1999 killed more than 20,000 people and 300,000 cattle, and damaged 2 million tonnes of paddy crop. Navdanya's community seed banks have mobilized seeds to rehabilitate agriculture and rebuild food security. For us in the Navdanya movement, conservation is not separate from production, and protecting biodiversity is not in conflict with meeting human needs.

We need to create new rules based on an inclusive freedom, rules based on compassion and the celebration of life's biodiversity, not narrow rules of commerce which commodify and colonize all life. Defending the freedom of others, and their rightful share to sustenance from the earth needs sensitivity to life in its myriad forms, and it requires full awareness of the impacts of our actions on other life forms. Localization is therefore an ethical imperative in an earth democracy, since only in local contexts can we assess and reduce our negative impact on other species. Localization requires reclaiming our self-organizing capacities as citizens and communities so that we also respect the self-organizing capacity and intrinsic worth of all bio-diversity. Trade rules need to be rewritten within the context of an earth democracy, and let biodiversity show us the way to the future. The future of biodiversity is after all our future. Tomorrow's biodiversity will shape the context for tomorrow's humanity. If biodiversity is threatened, our future as a human species and a human community is threatened. Our survival is intimately connected with other species. Both for their sake and ours we need to shift our focus rapidly from the current single-minded obsession with the global market to building and strengthening an earth democracy.

The conservation of biodiversity implies the freedom of all species to continue to live and evolve into the future, the freedom of the poor to have access to food and medicine, and the freedom of future generations to benefit from the bounties of living diversity. This inclusive freedom and liberation is what biodiversity offers us, and its future is in our hands.

Select Bibliography and Sources

Action Aid, *Astra Zeneca and its Genetic Research: Feeding the World or Fuelling Hunger*, London, 1999

Anderson, R. A., 'The Diversity of Eukaryotic Algae', in *Global Biodiversity*, Brian Groombridge (ed.), (Natural History Museum, London, and International Union for Conservation of Nature, IUCN), London, 1992

Baldwin, Paul, 'Monsanto Herbicide Could Damage Ecosystem', *Guardian*, London, 13 October 1999

Bandopadhyay, D. 'Food Security and Liberalization', paper, International Conference on Globalization of Agriculture and Growth of Food Security, New Delhi, 1996

Benbrook, Charles, 'Evidence of the Magnitude and Consequences of the Roundup Ready Soybean Yield Drag from University Based Varietal Trials in 1998', Ag. Biotech Info Net, Technical Paper No. 1, 13 July 1999

Bennett, Erna, 'Threats to Crop Plant Genetic Resources', in J. G. Hawkes (ed.), *Conservation and Agriculture*, London, 1978

Bondry, P., et al., 'The origin and evolution of weed beets: consequences for the breeding and release of herbicide-resistant transgenic sugar beets', *Theoretical Applied Genetics*, 87, 1993

Bray, Francesca, 'Agriculture for Developing Nations', *Scientific American*, July 1994

Brich, A. N. E., et al., 'Interactions between plant resistance genes, pest aphid populations and beneficial aphid predators', *Annual Report of the Scottish Crop Research Institute*, Dundee, 1996–97

Carson, Rachel, *Silent Spring*, Cambridge, Mass., 1962; London, 1963

Colinvaux, P., *Why Big Fierce Animals are Rare*, Harmondsworth, 1980

Cox, C., 'Glyphosate: Part I Toxicology, Herbicide Factsheet', *Journal of Pesticide Reform*, vol. 15, No. 3, Oregon, Fall 1995

—, W. S. Pease, et al., 'Preventing Pesticide Related Illness in Californian Agriculture', Environmental Health Policy Program Report, University of California, School of Public Health, Berkeley, 1995

Crick, H. G. P., et al., *Breeding Birds in the Wider Countryside: Their Conservation Status (1992–96)*, British Trust for Ornithology, January 1998

Dawkins, Richard, *The Selfish Gene*, Oxford, 1976

Dessee, Chris, 'Unnatural Selection or Bad Choice', *Wild Duck Review*, vol. v, No. 2, Nevada, Summer 1999

Dorfler, Wolfgang Kreissel, paper at 'Road to Seattle' seminar organized by Heinrich Böll Foundation, Washington, D.C., 21–22 Oct. 1999

Doyle, Jack, *Altered Harvest*, New York, 1985

Food and Agriculture Organization (FAO), United Nations , *Development Education Exchange Papers (DEEP)*, Sept. 1993

—, Fisheries Department, *The State of World Fisheries and Aquaculture*, Rome, 1995

—, 'Women Feed the World', 16 Oct. 1998

—, *World Watch List for Domestic Animal Diversity*, 5 Dec. 1995

Fowler, Cary, and Pat Mooney, *Shattering*, Tucson, Ariz., 1990

Gebaner, G., 'mRNA expression of components of the insulin-like growth factor system in breast cancer cell lines, tissues and metastatic breast cancer cells', *Anti-cancer Research*, 18: 2A, 1998

Goethe, J. W., *Scientific Studies*, Douglas Muller (ed.), Suhrkamp, N.Y., 1988

Gorman, T., 'Killer Bee', *Los Angeles Times*, 1 Nov. 1994

Greene, A. E., and R. F. Allison, 'Viruses and Transgenic Crops', *Science*, 263, 1994

Greenpeace and the Soil Association, *The True Cost of Food*, London, 1999

Groombridge, Brian, (ed.), *Global Biodiversity*, report compiled by the World Conservation Monitoring Centre (Natural History Museum, London, and IUCN), London, 1992

Hammand, B. G., et al., 'The feeding value of soy beans fed to rats, chicken, catfish, and dairy cattle is not altered by genetic incorporation of glyphosate tolerance', *Journal of Nutrition*, 1126 (3)

Hawkes, J. G. (ed.), *Conservation and Agriculture*, London, 1978

Hawkinson, S. E., et al., 'Circulating concentrations of insulin-like growth factor 1 and risk of breast cancer', *Lancet*, 351, London, 1998

Heywood, V. H., *Global Biodiversity Assessment*, Cambridge, 1995

Hilbech, A., et al., 'Toxicity of Bt. to the predator *Chrysoperla carnea*', *Environmental Ecology*, vol. 27, No. 4, Aug. 1998

Ho, Mae-Wan, *Genetic Engineering: Dream or Nightmare? The Brave New World of Bad Science and Big Business*, Bath and New Delhi, 1998

Holmes, M. T., et al., 'Effects of *Klepsiella planticola* on Soil Biota and Wheat Growth in Sandy Soil', *Applied Soil Ecology*, vol. 326, 1998

Holzman, David, 'Agricultural Biotechnology: Report leads to Debate on Benefits of Transgenic Corn and Soya Bean Crops', *Genetic Engineering News*, vol. 19, No. 8, New York, 15 April 1999

Iltis, H., 'Serendipity in Exploration of Biodiversity: What Good are Weedy Tomatoes', in E .O. Wilson (ed.), *Biodiversity*, Washington, D.C., 1986

International Association of Plant Breeders (ASSINSEL) 'Feeding the Eight Billion and Preserving the Planet', brochure, Chemin du Reposoir 7, 1260 NYON, Switzerland, 1998

Inose, T., and K. Murata, 'Enhanced accumulation of toxin (a case study on the safety of genetically engineered yeast)', *International Journal of Food Science Technology*, 30, 1995

Iyengar, A.K. Yegna, 'Field Crops of India', Bangalore BAPPCO, 1944 (reprinted 1980)

James, Clive, *Global Review of Commercialized Transgenic Crops*, International Society for Acquisition of Ag. Biotech Applications Briefs (ISAAA), Ithaca, N.Y., 1998

—, *Global Status of Transgenic Crops in 1997*, (ISAAA), Ithaca, N.Y., 1997

Jorgensen, R.B., and B. Anderson, 'Spontaneous Hybridization between oilseed rape (*Brassica napus*) and *B. campestriz* (Brassicaceae), *American Journal of Botany*, 1994

Kadir, Djelal, *Columbus and the Ends of the Earth*, Berkeley, Calif., 1992

Keenan, L., 'First Case of GMO Food Contamination', *Genetics Food Alert*, press release, 4 Feb. 1999

Keller, Evelyn Fox, *A Feeling for the Organism: The Life and Work of Barbara McClintock*, San Francisco, 1983

Kloppenburg, Jack, *First the Seed*, Cambridge, 1988

Koopowitz, Harold and Hilary Kaye, *Plant Extinction: A Global Crisis*, London, 1990

Lappé, Frances Moore, and Joseph Collins, *Food First*, London, 1982

Lappé, Marc, and Britt Bailey, *Against the Grain*, London, 1999

—, et al., *Journal of Medicinal Food*, vol. 1, No. 4, New York, 1998

Lewontin, Richard, *The Doctrine of DNA*, New York, 1993

Lyadyansky, M. L., D. McDonald and D. MacNiell, 'Impact of Zebra Mussel, a Bivalve Invader', *Bio-Science*, Sept. 1993

Mackenzie, Debora, 'Can We Really Stomach GM Foods?', *New Scientist*, London, 30 Jan. 1999

Millstone, E., E. Brunner and S. Mayer, 'Beyond Substantial Equivalence', *Nature*, vol. 401, 7 Oct. 1999

Mooney, P., 'From Cabbages to Kings, Intellectual Property vs. Intellectual Integrity', Proceedings of ICDA Conference on Patenting of Life Forms, Brussels, 1989

National Farmers Union, 'The Farm Crisis', paper presented to the Senate Standing Committee on Agriculture and Forestry, Ottawa, Feb. 18, 2000

Nestle, M., 'Allergies to Transgenic Foods: Questions of Policy', *The New England Journal of Medicine*, vol. 334, 11, 1996

Newman, Stuart, interview in *Wild Duck Review*, vol. v, No. 2, Nevada, Summer 1999

Nottingham, Stephan, *Eat Your Genes*, London, 1998

Ogutu-Ohwaya, R., 'Nile Perch in Lake Victoria', in Odd Sandlund, et al. (eds) *Invasive Species and Biodiversity Management*, Dordrecht, 1999

Organization for Economic Co-operation and Development (OECD), 'Safety Evaluation of Foods Derived by Modern Biotechnology', Paris, 1993

Outwater, J. C., et al., 'Dairy products and breast cancer: the IGF-1, estrogen and bgh hypothesis', *Medical Hypothesis*, 48, 1997

Pimental, David, et al., 'Economic and Environmental Benefits of Biodiversity', *Bio-Science*, Dec. 1997

Prescott-Allen, Robert and Christine, *Genes from the Wild*, London, 1983

Pretty, J., *Regenerating Agriculture*, Washington, D.C., 1995

Research Foundation for Science, Technology and Ecology (RFSTE), *Basmati Biopiracy*, New Delhi, 1998

—, *Monsanto: Peddling 'Life Sciences' or 'Death Sciences'*, New Delhi, 1998

—, 'Starving the Four Billion and Destroying the Planet: Myths of Industrial Breeding and Agricultural Biotechnology', briefing paper for biosafety negotiations, Convention on Biodiversity, Montreal, 14–17 May 1997

—, 'Speech by the President of Monsanto', 30 Oct. 1997, Forum on Nature and Human Society (US National Academy of Sciences, Washington, D.C.), New Delhi, 1998

Reuters, 'UK has new scare on genetic pollen spreading', 30 Sept. 1999

Rissler, Jane, and Margaret Mellon, *The Ecological Risks of Engineered Crops*, Cambridge, Mass., 1996

Rosset, Peter, and Miguel Altieri, 'The Productivity of Small-Scale Agriculture', International Forum on Agriculture White Paper, 1999

Royal Society for the Protection of Birds (RSPB), Press Release, London, 21 March 1999

Rural Advancement Foundation International (RAFI), *Gene Giants*, communiqué, March/April 1999

Schubbert, et al., 'Ingested foreign DNA survives transically in the gastrointestinal tract and enters the bloodstream of mice', *Molecular Genetics* 242

Shanti, George, *Operation Food*, Delhi, 1985

Shiva, Vandana, 'Betting on Biodiversity' (letter), RFSTE Policy Report, New Delhi, 1997

—, *Biodiversity: Social and Ecological Perspectives*, World Rainforest Movement, Penang, 1991

—, *Biodiversity-based Productivity*, New Delhi, 1996

—, *Ecological Costs of Economic Globalization: The Indian Experience*, New Delhi, 1997

—, *Monocultures of the Mind: Perspectives on Biodiversity and Biotechnology*, London, 1993

—, *Staying Alive: Women, Ecology and Development*, London, 1998

—, *The Violence of the Green Revolution*, London and Penang, 1991

— and Afsar H. Jafri, *Seeds of Suicide: The Ecological and Human Costs of Globalization of Agriculture*, New Delhi, 1998

—, Afsar H. Jafri and Ashok Emani, 'Globalization and the Threat to Seed Security', *Economic and Political Weekly*, Bombay, March 1999

—, and Ashok Emani, *Climate Change and the Orissa Cyclone*, New Delhi, 1999

—, and Gurpreet Karir, *Chemmeenkettu*, New Delhi, 1996

Strohman, Richard, interview in *Wild Duck Review*, vol. v, No. 2, Nevada, Summer 1999

Suzuki, David, and Holly Dressel, *From Naked Ape to Super Species*, Toronto, 1999

Swaminathan, M. S., *Science and the Conquest of Hunger*, Delhi, 1983

Thrupp, L. A., 'New Partnerships for Sustainable Agriculture', World Resources Institute (WRI), 1997

Traavik, Terje, 'An Orphan in Science: Environmental Risks of Genetically Engineered Vaccines', Report No. 1999-6, Directorate of Nature Management, Trondheim, 1999

Tudge, Colin, *The Engineer in the Garden*, London, 1993

UNDP, *Agroecology: Creating the Synergism for Sustainable Agriculture*, 1995

Update on Risk Research, 'Process Counts', *The Gene Exchange*, Washington, D.C., Fall/Winter, 1998

US Academy of Sciences, 'Field Testing Genetically Modified Organisms', Washington, D.C., 1989

Vellvé, Renée, *Saving the Seed: Genetic Diversity and European Agriculture*, London, 1992

Wilson, E.O. (ed.), *Biodiversity*, Washington, D.C., 1986

Woolf, Marie, *Independent*, London, 18 April 1999

Worcester, Tracy, *Resurgence*, Hartland, Devon, March/April 2000

Index